THE ROCKING CHAIR

The Rocking Chair

BRADLEY J. FEST

BLUE SKETCH PRESS

BLUE SKETCH PRESS
8 Mellon Terrace
Pittsburgh, PA 15206
www.bluesketchpress.com

Copyright 2015 by Bradley J. Fest

All rights reserved, including right of reproduction in whole or in part or in any form.

Printed in the United States of America
9 8 7 6 5 4 3 2 1
First Printing, Blue Sketch Press Trade Paperback Edition, 2015
ISBN (print)   978-1-942547-02-0
ISBN (ebook)   978-1-942547-03-7

Cover Art by Taylor Baldwin, *U.S. Infantry Camel Corps (feat. Emma Lazarus)*. More information available at www.taylorbaldwinstudio.com
Design by Little Owl Creative, www.littleowlcreative.com
Edited by Joseph N. Welch, III.

ACKNOWLEDGEMENTS
Some of these poems have appeared in *PELT*, *After Happy Hour Review*, *Flywheel Magazine*, *Bath House*, *Open Thread Regional Review*, and *Spork*.

In memory of my father

CONTENTS

Making Anxiety Fun	xi
Preface/Prologue: The Summation of Problems/the Posing of Questions	1
First Interlude/Apologia	6
I. Gambit and Zero Hour	7
[The Last Chance Saloon]	
A. Dung Beetle of Love	8
B. The Unroll(-Up)	12
i.	
ii.	
iii.	
iv.	
v.	
vi.	
II. A. i. The One	15
[Symphony of the Great Transnational	
I.	
II. After Racing to the Engineer's Room, Dodging Bullets, and Leaping the Gaps Between the Cars	
III.	
IV.	
V.]	
ii.	
B. Two Parts of a Parallax Gap	26
i. After the Dance	
ii. The Apocalypse Archive	
III. A. Three Months, the Ship Is Waiting	30
B. i. Effluvium	35
ii. A Second E(ff)luvium	38
IV.	41
A. Meditations on the Diabolic	43
i. Prelude for the Devil	
ii. For the Infernal Pit Shall Never Hold Celestial Spirits in Bondage	44

	iii. *Die Götterdämmerung, oder, den Spiegel vorhalten?*	45
	iv. Definitely Not Advice. It Comes from the Divel, the True Master and Giver of Such Rapture	46
	v. A Statue of the Destroyer Lies Beneath Layers of Salt	47
	vi. The Code Is Just as Unwieldy Upside Down	48
	vii. In that Hour of Gentleness	49
B. Blame		50

V. Evening and Morning, Drunkenness and Dreaming — 53
    A. The Baseball Description — 54
        [Intermission/Second Interlude] — 56
        i. The Retired Cobb — 58
    B. Late in the Twenty-Seventh Inning — 59

VI.   A.   i. Nautilus or Plotinus — 60
            ii. Volcanoes/Organics — 61
            iii. If the Marianas Trench Were a Gathering of Sound — 63
            iv. The Path of . . . — 64
            v. An Unlikely and Heretofore Unseen Calm — 65

VII. Oceanic: Theses on the Abuses of Indexicality (A Narrative of the Hyperarchive) — 66
    A. Oceanic
    B. Indexicality — 67
    C. IOPT — 69
    D. Don't Sweat the Small Stuff: Burn the Fucking Library — 71
    E. A Not Too Thinly Veiled Critique Against the Ametascientific "Newness" — 72
    F. Saguaro — 74
    G. Access: Denied — 75
    H. Ode to the Quadratics of Soprano-Voiced Mathematicians — 77
    I.   i.   a. Future Journal — 80
                b. Recently Discovered! Pre-Consolidation Auto-Analog-Bio Found!
        i.½
        ii.
    J. To Imagine the Radically Other — 82
    K. The Deca(y)des — 83
    L. From DNA to CNN — 84

		M. Nothingness Introduced into the Heart of the Image	85
VIII.	A.		86
		i. a.	
		1.	
		b.	
	B. there is only one possible TitlE		88
	C. Confession Fermata		90
	D.		91
		[Footnote 59]	
IX.			96
	A.		99

Afterword/Postlude: New Problems in the Synchronic, New
    Questions for the Haptic, the Spatial, the Festering Body   100

Appendix I   101

Appendix II   107

Endnotes   109

    Oceanic II   112
    Conversation Among the Ruins
    Yet Another Destroyer and the Tale of that Destruction
        (In the First Person)   113

Acknowledgments   117

»Siehe, sprach ich weiter, diesen Augenblick! Von diesem Torwege Augenblick läuft eine lange ewige Gasse rückwärts: hinter uns liegt eine Ewigkeit.

Muß nicht, was laufen kann, *von allen Dingen, schon einmal diese Gasse gelaufen sein? Muß nicht, was geschehn* kann, *von allen Dingen, schon einmal geschehn, getan, vorübergelaufen sein?*

Und wenn alles schon dagewesen ist: was hältst du Zwerg von diesem Augenblick? Muß auch dieser Torweg nicht schon—dagewesen sein?

Und sind nicht solchermaßen fest alle Dinge verknotet, daß dieser Augenblick alle *kommenden Dinge nach sich zieht? Also——sich selber noch?*

Denn, was laufen kann *von allen Dingen: auch in dieser langen Gasse* hinaus*—muß es einmal noch laufen!«*

Friedrich Nietzsche, *Also sprach Zarathustra*

THE ROCKING CHAIR[1, 2]

---

[1] **Making Anxiety Fun**

This is the clarion call we offer (nothing else);
this is that moment between whether to switch sides
or change the record. It is that small space
in which a dung beetle of love can roll on
unimpeded, where we can kick the goddamn chair
and send it back on its way, where, if you look closely enough,
you'll be able to see a few owl pellets, a few singularities
to be dismantled into their constituent parts;
and if it is not these things, well, it is merely something else.

If I were to go out every evening drinking intellectually for the rest
of my time in Attica, well, I'd make it a plan
to make anxiety fun, to be sure to talk
about the apocalypse and the fact that my mom was a nun;
and if in the quotidian experiment in which the thermodynamic
fact that hats are occasionally worn backwards has the potential
to create mountains of glorious pellet-fur completely inundated with
small moments of perfectly triangulated—in an isosceles manner—
days of Sodom . . . and if you were to let the world
only hide its hideous face underneath rags of
GERD . . . if you were to let it tuck its phallic sheath into quotients of
letting the motionless cigarette burn its way down with hanging ash,
well, then, I'd say that the moment of tomorrow was actually back
on this plane long enough to hear that *today*
is the greatest day of my life.
And it would hopefully be something that I could tell
genealogical midgets the timing belt story of a different Pop's life.
If it were all these things, I'd be able to consciously recognize "Silver"
as only one concrete object, an object that, if it were not for its infamous
non-notoriety, would not receive its just due as the only moment of
non-reification that is craved. So come on,
let someone croon you to sleep
while the Pharaoh of your last cognitive step
lets infinity into your dreams so that all you'd've had would be
merely an ending, which can never be anything except a beginning.

[2] One of the principle heirlooms I have inherited, but do not and can never in any way possess, is this chair. It was thought never to be stable. It stayed in rhythm with the spinning earth, the minute tectonic invasions, the breath of walls, our own—small though it may be—gravity.
If no one were to sit in it. . . .

It stops.
        That chair, your rocking chair father, it stops.

Preface/Prologue: The Summation of Problems/the Posing of Questions

How much time we have wasted.
Whether it be the tripping indeterminacy of sound/seconds,
        that whittling away while fall minute-hours,
        an *Agaetis byrjun* of years, of eons,
                      on the backyard
                      porch swing or
        a return to that station only every seven years,
        the rest condemned to that lonely prairie ride. . . .
Whatever it be, there is not a single moment that is truly
        accounted for,
    no *now* to spring faultless into cold calm and responsibility,
        drinking unquenchably from the pure spirit of spring.
How much time we have wasted.

Much dancing was to be had on those Percocet evenings:
time like a dandy roar in a dime store,
we, with shirt tucked and shiny shoes,

let the train-tracks be our wine-stop, our stomachs
wasted in South Tucson.
How much time we wasted crawling our bellyful selves into that
        dawn of shattered crystal in darkness.

        Yet, we could call ourselves resplendent,
        that's the rub. This echo-soft down we live
        is not static matter; there is the unreliable, the changing
        wavelengths not provided for by any of our senses,
        these blank spots of cornea damage.[a]

    The problem is not something laid easy-bare, skin and testicles
        hanging on lab coats . . .
    and yet it lies in the ability to define and confirm byway the
        negative.
    That old yarn of accentuate the positive:
    good advice if you go for that "fullness of being" effect,
    lying prone and naked, slowly rubbing your chest to keep cool.

How much time *have* we wasted?
The slough-off grinding that awaits our hands every morning
of that "what-to-do-today"—of that expectation requiring responsibility,

duration, dictation, that crapshoot of what we will here call free will
(for lack of a better term, for lack of—scintillating 1968—a glimmer
of Paris at possibly one last sanguine yearning) and intestine-body-
      dreaming
defeats. How much time we have wasted.

A phrase: "the victory of consciousness has never been close at hand,"
would require refutation if it were not so horribly true, if this whole thing
had not gone so horribly wrong.
And yet to even proclaim one way or another
requires some method. And I, for one,
am sick of methods.[b]
So where does one begin, where does the accent fall on that great
      engendering note?
Before or after
some titanic mind packed up its belongings
and left this sphere for greener-waste-pastorals (and is there any logic
or any answer in cactus-strewn desert)?
One would like to think so,
to think that if someone dug deep enough,
stretched whatever hand tools
to their liminal expedience,
that there would be some governing trace
below thick layers of crust and oil, some quicksand discovery of skull
or bonnet, maybe supercomputer still functioning archaeologic
despite tectonic shifting. And maybe this would be a mirror.

I deny that the problem is because   words are so miserable.
    Undulating pastness stampedon every one.
    Cryptograms and cephalic vaingloriousness.
    These moments arrive
        to be lost on their way to "this remote corner of the universe"[c]
where language stumbles always, yet picks itself up again if only
to scream "why!?"[3] at the heavens and fall back in on itself, treading
paths lonely-crowded and bubbled-molten-searing. Once, everything
was fire. If there has been any change, "Absolute Zero" is the cause,
      surely, for explanations stumble haphazard by deistic
      waywardness. Can we do nothing but forge ahead? Picking ice-
      stubble out of the illusory and hammering at it (sadly only
      another hammer is inside, the same hammer)? Saturnalia on the
      road to incomplete frescoes?

---

[3] Or quite possibly "who!?"

I propose that maybe the correct posing of no method at all is to take Mr. Lynch at his word and to follow those strange alien broad-feeders in their tracks, a quick tune, and then to be lodged in this feather-bed. . . . With the pure push toward transcendence and eschatology from intertwining actual historical documentation with completely fictionalized events (such as positing a self-portrait of Jung), the historical lets eternity and transcendence enter unflinchingly because it can never be the truth. Thus the Hollywood historical drama is closer to the actual working of history upon the subject, despite its inauthentic nature, than a historian calling out the inauthentic nature of the object in question. And much like waking from a dream, when one exits the theater, the "painting" in the film (or in this case, the poem) will resonate because a) it was *there*, b) there was no one *there* to deauthenticate it, and c) it resonates with history by the very fact of its pure fictionality. The Plan: an eschatology is quite possibly necessary: the veil of *māyā* pulled over, the illusion that leads one into life, in a Nietzschean sense. It becomes history's task, whether it knows it or not, to create the veil, not to deauthenticate the veil, but to authenticate what is very much not *there* anymore. (Seriously though, if I found out a film did actually exist with Carl Jung in a room with his self-portrait, I would probably have a breakdown. It would cut all the cords.)[4]

---

[4] This is not (and brings us to the question of voice.
It is extremely important to remember that
time is not an issue here, there is none of it to be wasted.
The limit between one language and the next is not aural
but a mere spatial distortion on the fabric of our bookshelf.
We will be *Highly Refined Pirates** and nothing will not be sitting,
waiting, begging, and drooling for this splendid plundering.
Whew, glad that's out of the way!) an apology.

*Minus the Bear. Probably best known round these parts for the best praise any person could possibly hope to receive: [he/]she, this girl[/boy] can drink well; *and* their wide ranging witticisms for song titles: "**Absinthe**† party at the [infinite mildew] warehouse," "we are not a football team," "damn bugs whacked him, Johnny," and "thanks for the killer game of Crisco® twister."

†We retreat from what feels
like destiny. I feel nothing. I will flow from something living dying
breathing in our heart's monotony.

I will be completely honest with you right now. I am not a man. I am
a figment of imagination.

I tried to feel once
and it lost itself
in an incandescent
work-order. Relieving from the very basis of things,
we set upon night and wake all the mystifying imbalance toward the

I give it all up. I surrender my faces to the wind[5]
and ask, so, should we not concern ourselves with which gods we are
        reborn as?
In fact, it is quite amazing how loud the host is when it comes to those
        questions.
Quite, how shall we say, quite "so much, upon us all a little rain must
        fall?"
In the history of everything, I
am not afraid to be fearless and tell you right now in simple language that
        . . .

and cum again *and* let me tell you about my *Decameron* t(h)rill?

And when she walks, she walks. She looks me in the eye.
One in every three parts is no information
whatsoever. Those people we scowl at,
they really are the beautiful ones;
and then there are others. Other, which one (that blooming *Solaris*),
or one that we could half-easily call her?
Should not she know by now it's either coffee[d] or
nicotine that brings the truly Coleridgean mistakes upon
the most lucid of night=screams?
And the problem truly is
that you do not want to have to shoot your way out of anything.

If only I could feed Torches to Rome a decent biscuit, merely for respect,
        if only—there
when you better watch your back. If only.
Some . . . no I'll keep quiet, no moonshine for you, dear somnambulist,
        dear loverly lady. . . .

Come soon traitor.
Claim your diligence in the aftereffect of your desert.
I am actually feeling something, so
call the Central Brain for certain shoque troops
to replenish the ranks: there are no questions. My dreams tell me this.
The story must begin soon, elsewhyse—
the crowd. (Is it all critique?)

---

        truth of things.
    We will all halt at our very center.

[5] Potentially.

No, I am beginning a journey through Kentucky
and it is there in a little chapel,
a transferred historic period piece, where this story, this quest(ion),[6]
which is only and always the story of this nation
(and thus a love story as well), begins.

---

[6] Which is, of course, Cronos himself wielding his self-dooming bough, lurking through tactile halls diurnally, forgetting the parallel-planed-mirrors, the light, the refraction, and the equation, the Casimir Effect: the fluctuations of a vacuum, the nothing, the Ø, and the set surrounding it (really can make something out of nothing, oh god/fathertime).

[First Interlude/Apologia[7]:

I know it would be silly of me here to ask for forgiveness, but I must apologize for the grandiosity and grandiloquence of the opening section, even the relative incoherence. To even begin to approach my task I felt it necessary to go for the throat (of existence) immediately and then look around, get my bearings, see where I was. I felt this was completely necessary at the time, but obviously have reconsidered since this apology is coming so early. So lay back, have a cigarette, it is about to begin (for real).]

---

[7] *This is.*

> (This city *is not* a wick.
> Hanford and Bellona, those cities, *are*.)

I. Gambit and Zero Hour

How much time I have wasted
>asking who amongst my brethren, my kin deserves that throne, its wooden arms bitten and clawed by infants and children of one great progenitor. There was no estate sale. No auction or hearing. Not even a manner of lion-hearts or long-shanks, least of all that coveting swampy generation.

No, it was not a low moment, not an indeterminate crushing and self-
>imposed cataracting—no hubris could prevent my veins standing out to feel the razors running rapid inside—up and down, up and down.

Whatever pilgrimage had begun, whether escaping plague or descending
>Aquinian, the cresting horizon of red and gold on a field of blue, star in the center looking best from a great height, it was an opening into, a constant re-inscription of linear calumny, but also a succession.

To begin, to be taken in by moving away toward heat and abstract body-
>bent dreaming, cannot be purely movement. For what appears simple and defined, chord-like in its unified field, no theory can string together its disparate and discordant shades, its massive yearning lying fallow to wait on buttressed amalgamation and knowledgeable stillness.[8]

Ashen mouth, reattach my forgotten narrative, my forgotten hard minutes
>at **The Last Chance Saloon**.[9, 10, e]

---

[8] When I emerged from praying
to a sign, "Be still and know,"
at Patti's 1880s settlement in
Western Kentucky, the cock crowed immediately
when I exited the chapel,
then twice more that siren call of emergence sounded. A cat mewed thrice as well,
and now neither cat nor rooster can stop their racket.
I had not prayed since Saint Paul's in London eight years ago,
and I could say that all of them were answered then.

Today I asked permission for the Earth to stay this way
forever, to never be engulfed in the flame of rapture,
which took much humbling on my part to even begin
to lay at the foot of the doors and knock with a kiss.
>—Patti's 1880s settlement, off the parkway in Kentucky, about thirty miles from Paducah.

[9] I wish I could say that it had been a cold night,
that a dark wind had howled against the shutter of the windows,
that she had not come home yet, but had been due hours ago,
that I had begun preparing a prayer. I cannot.
The power had gone out.

¹⁰ There was a part of myself that once desired to demand—
in parts of itself, undulating and individuating—: *take us to the threshold.*
Do not ask wherefore it went;
suffice it to say,
the whiskey's calm tonight.

Once called a haze,
it's running sidecar.

The years once taken off
are rediscovered in glacially eroded
sonic patterns, sitting so dormant
on a shelf for years.
This will move toward the crystals
that chill our refreshing beverage

of exorcising the past's hold (not stranglehold)
on the things that, circling above but tied to a string,
keep tracing their (re-)inscribed paths—
a massive cutting in which gravity eases its tyranny:
distanceless icebergs giving their bulk to the sky.

A. Dung Beetle of Love

Rolling ball of Myrmidons gathering every single object
in-path-weariness, what will be left after this becoming, this coming
singularity[11] but a *Katamari Damacy*, but a putting of kings to death,
a plucking of alacritous institutions, a punishment of that prince's dearth
and incomparable sumptuousness?[f]

O tragically fated *Rex Nemorensis*, what spritely water nymph could not
    escape
your (h)orrific[umbert] (h)abitation[umbert] and grasp your faultingly clear
    perspicacity
of what it means to be young, to be possessed by that easy god of
    engendering power,
that lush and ripe pregnancy for which all are fated in their own certain
    manner?

Dine on. The interruption that has waited so expectantly slathering in the
    hall
has corrupted itself into these guests' soup bowls. With clarion ease,
    blaring brightly,
the trumpet-call has put a stop to the parade of ceremonial events, a liquid
    plug
for this shower drain of festivity. Dine on.
For you would wait for some pronouncement?
For is it very true that there has been redrawn on the façade of that
    mansion y'all would enliven so brilliantly
with song and dance, a new sort of street-map, the windows: new
    buildings, the brick: new superhighways?
The test subjects are lying low in their humble abodes, sipping coffee
    drinks
and working new esotericisms in the frowning moment of servile
    enjoyment.
This is not a test. This is. This fountain of self-made acceptance, of self-
    quieting disrupture
painted quiet, burden-like on steamed iciness, we would like to ask a
    question.
Sad and temporally fated meanderings, for what purchase do you claim
    any hold upon the ground of discomfort? Peopled and easy sing-
    song falling,
when does this party stop, where does one exit this train for seven year

---

[11] What, except Gödel's Incompleteness Theorem?

    mistaken identity?

The bathroom is down the hall and to the left.
There, it is marked with symbols of bounty and harvest.
Oh, the simple strain that marks a good reaping and sowing, please
do not mistake the complete lack of anything whatsoever, branching,
undulating, frying its sweet pangs of autumnal crises, for this: not
    forsooth a kind of dreaming
and this is, if under swaying elm and willow the calls of kites and hound-
    dogs,
baying at the corpse for which some protection will not let them eat of its
    legendary limbs—
all for naught do we mistake gay Metropoli for their savage protectors,
    their blue and red
flapping against backgrounds of the most vile and cruel combat, most
    bloody and nameless war.
The image of things. The image of this most specific thing, so inscribed as
    to be nameless
and yet holding its functioning sway, all streams eventually leading back to
    their source,
these parents of generations, these origins, this new kind of genealogy.
    Are not these
specifications aptly applied to what has been ordered, selected carefully
    from the catalog
of clamoring multiplicity? Rosebud of the workshop, peeled softly
in the delicate backroom where everything is crafted accordingly,
not a breath left but to utter that phantasm: reason itself does not err.
[~Pr(g) if and only if G is not provable (4). g=GN(~Pr(g)) -
X∞X: the license plate of the most notorious Ø-edger.]
Mega-gargantuan-lopolis, read here your sweet call to Eurydice's side. The
    ruse is up.
There is no longer any necessity to resist the quiet temptation of
    destruction.
Troy's sweet walls were always meant to fall; it was fated by the gods,
and there is absolutely no complaining allowed. Fusseth-noteth. Lean
    back in your easy chair
and light the pipe of sweet careful tobacco seeds and smoke in that dying
    moonlight, amber
on the eastern horizon as it rises to blood-big brilliance, a cautious
    entrance hanging for viewing Truman's pathetic tale. On display.
    A mannequin. A harlotry disguised as the vaguest.
Walk those sweet hams of thighs up these stairs. This is not a request.
And for these simple demands I will comb the steppe of Rockies

and banks of Styx, eager to forget ponderous afflictions of erratum.
Reason does not. . . .

What a crying journey I have made of my life.[12] I wish you had been
    there to see it.
To offer a slice of advice, for this, your most wayward of sitters. At this
    very moment
I seem bent and intent on letting you pass to an older, more fitted initiate,
    but most
mean you for me. The placard of your previous inhabitant lies as a
    brushing insult
upon ground meant for and holding others. I had nothing to do with that.
    I promise.
So I will bellow an incantation and wait for the divine order of rulers to
    let me sit calmly in that so splendid of thrones. The one forgotten
    and left dormant when sugary weakness claimed a life, a glorious
    and most important existence.
Trauerarbeit is a life's occupation.[13]

---

[12] I always forget I am Catholic—what strange inborn will toward confession.
[13] The work of mourning or mourning-work.

B. The Unroll(up)

i.

    And oh what hearkens in the west?
              A no fun call out of the signal blast, out of the
        crises a-paranoia, *a fortiori* the calmest of non-beings. Just
              inside the ruins
    we come to pale faced ones of the worst kind of kicking.

ii.

    That filling station
    pride of souring
    at the prostitute's side.

    Everything has been rolled into a giant ball.
    The circumference does not quite reach my sides.
    World without end.

    A half-naked woman may lie before me and I could not grok.
    This is form-line.
    And this is not

    that crawling underhandedness that it so obviously attests to.
    The bed calls and I am weeping

iii.

    drams of city-glass on the formica floor,
    waiting light-box hallucinations of the last time.

iv.

    Let us see. Cinquefoil? Right. Cinema vérité. No. That wasn't it at all. Cipher. Looks like that's the one. Yes: "a) a system of secret writing based on a key, or set of predetermined rules or symbols."[g]

    [And it is amazing: I'm not burning my hair off. I *will* be the first and last to know. I've driven across Texas too.]

    I am afraid that the manner we converse with each other is only the dimmest memory of our having lived on Olympus.

Good ole' Fibonacci will save us. And yet . . . he does not have the key. If he did it would be all a dame-bastard dance at the prom, at the initiation. Nor do I. . . .

Nor do I.

v.

1, 1, 2, 3, 5, I declare a thumb war. On myself no less.[h]
Because I would not rather be with an animal.

Young boy violins. Center of attention.
Got a . . . fact I got two.

vi.

The mattress that I've hidden my hands in
has dissolved, frittered away by its own incontinence,
and I am at the height of some sordid, yet fallow ambience.
Music is howling over the moor, crying its sweet moment of
    jubilation,
laughing at my quivering hands, collecting my conscience; away
the swaddling child opens hands and maiden head as it rears the
    fold of skull
and brain meat into this infernal tassel, all might and august
    grandeur.
Bladder born, white like an angel's organs spilled on the street
    and soil
of these crises, these moment of dark spots reeling their
    abdomen—something
was born of me this morning, some terrible forgetting. As if
I had been touched of cornucopia dreaming once some years ago;
the mind, a plaything of Sisyphus, reclaims its own broiling
    amnesia,
its own inconstant invitation to drained remembering. There is
    nothing left
with which to soil myself in the white noise of morning: the sight
    of it
is like a heaven-sent mist upon my eyes, almost mistaken for rain
    or visible humidity,
but like the last story told in the afterthought of deistic architects.
    I moved against it
and returned, returned to the haunted landscapes of this night on
    Earth.

> Where once I grasped the steel rod of existence by holding both
> ends as parallel
> with a sphere as one can, the tangent broke off though
> adamantine, a wolf's cry
> in the distant hunt, the metamorphosis of sibilant acrostics,
> wordplay and thunder.[14]

---

[14] A year of fallen poets once raged about this earth like the perfect melody of suicide. One Giambatta Biambimbisti (1467-139? . . . like Mr. P. D. Q., his dates have been thoroughly corrupted by far too much scholarship) recorded the whole insanity with ultimate care, but also the most violent schizophrenia of fever and malaria. The poem had been lost until 1981, when one young scholar, Frank Haltings, unearthed it pasted between the leaves of some ancient folio in the library at the University of Southwestern Arizona A & P. The folio has since been burned by far too romantic undergraduates (with peculiar access to the Rare Book Room, I might add . . .), hoping to bring back the poor departed spirit of Giambatta; so any significance the folio had has vanished into the proverbial *æther*. Strangely and coincidentally, even though the poem was widely published as a thing of pure incandescent wonder, all copies have been lost except for the one here (roughly translated):

> Daub the corners of this silent emission, flaxen yet a yawping maw,
> frozen like blazed martyrs, burned into the iris of the past, crystallized, eternal.
> Hours of trappings descending forlorn in the mum-blazed Pythagoras. This
> room.
> This crazed habitation of birth, these sheets, and the bed-flowers parting the
> curtains
> through which peeping-eyed-tom(b)s let their will flow out of themselves,
> peppering the walls with sulfuric palisades, blood by all accounts, distraught and
> distinct
> myth-making jaundice. Sic the slathering and lost dogs of history upon the
> monads held-
> up, hellacious fibrils of the fabric of meaning and slack-jawed, cardinal-eyed
> management
> of this farcical realism, this central station of terrorized language.

[Sadly added to this are some almost indecipherable and horrible lines by some anonymous pseudo-poet, an innocuous defacement, a supreme defilement of this poem. It has become, however, impossible to read this poem without reading this cancerous addition, this impotent mumbling of someone, no one, some mistake of history only known for this tripe.]

> The dust kicked up in this useless attic, entirely stuffed with incomparably lost
> memory,
> has the distinct smell of . . . not corpses . . . but the formidable lichen that grows
> on the speed of light. As if the viceroy of catapulted lords and ladies has
> returned
> with his defenestrating corpuscular blindness, a bastion of tired [indecipherable].

[Though this may not be it at all. I have taken some liberty in attempting to read these indecipherable words, and amidst the mistakes there may be in the original, some semblance of beauty. . . .]

II.

A.i. The One

We had time enough to exit the sanctuary before the reformatting hit,
enough to spread a blanket of protection, small
to avoid the satellite-eye, before all we had built
became verdant-green-grass-pastoral. We had little choice at that point.
Phoenix by midnight . . . or the crowds would surround us
and demand
what was in our trunk,
what was causing this punishment,
this judgment.

We had found a One frozen solid in Paleolithic technology—
an early form of carbonite freeze.
Just about the time revolvers were still
the trick-of-the-trade, this stranger strangled
herself in immortal sleep, unwittingly awaiting this most ominous of days,

this time-of-times, this intrusion.
Her story is still sketchy at best,[15]

---

[15] **Symphony of the Great Transnational**

I.

Finally! The shift had occurred!
We had been stalled for days rocking worry on our haunches,
muttering about bandits, but now we were finished waiting
for that interminable freighter to pass—that long serpent
raking its claws against steel veins.
The tracks had shifted and we were on our way, chugging west,
the rain falling in a complex rhythm
with the steady cadence of forward moving wheels.
I hadn't smelled creosote since

gods with hammers, strange men from the east,
and overseers enough to disturb any union head
drove the last golden spike through. I can remember
being on that team all through that mottled Utah May,
up there in Promontory thanking Abe, who,
despite being mixed up with that kin problem,
had the foresight way back in '62
(a terrible year by all accounts,
my own being a yarn spun so thick and long
I'd have to ask ole' Munny for the exact details)

to give me that terrible job of connecting
two sides of an entity gobbling itself
like some reified behemoth
addicted to ether and loose women,
crawling slowly inward on its belly
of broken glass scales, weighing
the soil down with the disinterred hearts in its stomach
of the men and women who had fought
to keep that connection possible.

I had fought a little for both sides,
played the guest at some dirty gulag in El Paso,
and even sang professionally at a few state funerals,
but the Union Pacific had offered the only work
where I got three square meals.

Missing those fasts in my break,
afflicted with fever, dehydration:
the black death of the frontier . . .

the dining car rhymed with pity that day, the pity we all felt
sitting there, holding our hats, vigorously trying to ignore the whiskey haze.
I'm telling you, this was before refrigeration,
long before ice could exist in July on the Wyoming plain rushing by

(another
life, one might say today, but real,
like a movie projected on the side
of a warehouse, a storehouse
of jetset goods set to explode
when the bug hits the millennial fan—beef jerky
was the party program, our *raison d'être*, our yup
in the face of the vast unity of blue that hung above us.
Ole' Butch couldn't contain us—forward momentum!—
that forever western push doesn't succumb to the raids
of some blue-eyed, smooth talkin', well . . .
Yankee—never does. Keeps going.
Ole' world hadn't known frontiers in so long
that young Alex was still having the taws played upon—
that is all we have known. For centuries now.
So much distance and time and promises,
and of course we would always be separated by

ten thousand years and a vial of aspirin,
which mean photographs, which mean slide-shows
on a sheet of papyrus, which is nothing
sitting beside an anthill).

Nervous,
I poked my head out the engineer's side
two miles before the forest, smoothed my wrinkled chinos

(slightly dry, a momentary abundance—restless eyes,
helminth feet and a vague awareness
of being; closets stuffed full, citizens in their homes;
no song is ever good enough
except the gun blasts blinking against the glare
of falling ice to the north and a few John Henrys
who've forgotten Panatlanticism as soon as it began:
it split their heart).
This was the Great Transnational (that never
got off the ground). This would be
the liminal edge and end of the world, the end of Liberty Valance,
the end of tributaries actually feeding rivers
at this end of the tracks (there's good shopping,
good half-ravers in techno bars).
We were all stealing,
that's why I'm here—all those new friends,
here, in the west where every ounce of tweed
became a filial attachment—where—

where was paradise?

Outside my window
two bison roamed the Kansas plain
twirling semiotic batons
in the noon graylight. The men in the car
couldn't get to their guns fast enough.
Heard once that this sort of thing
was encouraged; sometimes the trains had to
come to a full stop for the herds. Heard once
that this sort of thing made one
believe we were all being led
somewhere. Heard it from

a little man with intense eyes
who told me about the epic
being written on the plains,
in the Rockies, and on the coasts.
That this epic was a tale
that would one day be told by silver light
in dark rooms and be seen by men, women, and children alike,
voyeurs who would remain completely motionless.
Word had gotten around to the right people,
so we added just a little bit each night
to this vast tale. It would be the tale
of the West, of times
when the rattlesnake posed the greatest threat
to running drugs out of Nogales.
But we gave it up. Trains have no tales,
only songs.

Closed, my eyes covered themselves naturally

amidst the gunfire, as if a dance of Sanskrit motion
combing the paths to the quarantined areas of this vast left
were the somewhere hinted at crying in the basement. If I
had gone down the steps to see just how high the watermark ran
during monsoon imago, I would have only seen the tracks running by,
which would force my body to lurch back into the sway
of the left-right, which would force my body topside,
where the watermark hadn't been seen in three generations.

Something about the movement of the train,
the steam whistle, the heat and dust
of the dining car, the fever of movement,
change, vision—something caused
the waiter and myself simultaneously
to whisper, "The shame."
The same something that disabled us
from glimpsing the other's whispered words
or the shadows of seagulls migrating east:
bleak shapes in the noontime sun.

Someone once told me in El Paso
that you could read an entire almagest
in the patterns of birds' shadows.
He, like the rest of us there,
was chained and hadn't seen
shadow since the trading company
put us there to rot for blowing open
cathedrals. Someone once told me
that this was the only pilgrimage . . . left,
always; I had a destination, with a name
and a face seen only on paper, which
made me very glad to see

that someone had been possessed
of enough foresight to put a player-piano
in one corner of the car. The tinkling keys
went well with the dusty whiskey symphony,
the sweat dripping from my forehead onto
the dry beef, and the obviously peculiar stare

of One-Eyed Jack: most notorious
cattle rustler in the territories:
my staked claim, all forest and ocean,
Oregon (for the uninitiated).

Sauntering over in step with the music,
I saw he was playing seven-card with a few cowboys,
their faces all stone and ice, twisted around the smoke
of each man's foul cigar. I pulled
the cigar from the nearest rustler's creased face to light my own,
and placing it back, said, "You One-Eyed Jack?" All heads turned slowly.

Jack leaned back in his chair and cocked his one good eye at me,
letting it linger on my pistol for a moment and said,
"Who's asking?" his voice like gravel rattling
in an empty tin drum riddled with bullet-holes.
"Well that depends," I said, while the cowboys
inched away from the table, "I can either be
your lovely escort for the evening, all done up
in ball gown and glass slippers, waiting
with patient hand for a waltz toward our destination,
or I can be the grim reaper of big-time end of the world
type eschatology, raining fire like the worst Abaddon."

"I see," he said, the cowboys now out of their seats, four of them,
and nothing between me and the door but a few loudmouthed
Easterners, their bladders already loosening. "You see miss,
there are a few words I'd like to have with any man or woman who comes along
looking for my hand or head, so if you don't mind,
before we start our mambo, listen well.

"Fever crystallized doesn't depend upon the sharpness of its points
but upon the breach it can make in the hull
of our Madeleine Ferguson memory.
Like breaking an arm, the old adage regarding loss
doesn't begin to clarify, only ease
the stop and go of Heraclitean flux:

"*This* is where I live.
A fieldmouse, a sandstorm off the port bow—this
is a lusty haven for the newly indicted,
the newly fixed for the always acquainted front line mongrels.

"This is where I roam dusty train tracks.
Goodbye lonely shipping yards,
the mustard stew has flown the coop
and we are all readying ourselves
for the goodbye fantod of crystals crystals."

II. **After Racing to the Engineer's Room, Dodging Bullets, and Leaping the Gaps Between the Cars**

The waxen glow of the fire
revealed gnarled hands too young to be
slowly stoking the flames with bent back
and a poker of hair. The man illumined
had fashioned tools from his beard
and gray hairs. So stoking the flame
became a slow, olfactory consumption,
an impotent burning, a slow hallucination.

The fumes from the hair brought him visions:
women strumming thick chords on motley guitars given at birth;

bartenders talking on cordless phones in a mad nexus of blues, reds;
visions of overwhelming youth, times when each petty tragedy,
each stirring moment, led to an outpouring.

As the man's poker slowly burned, his hand began to blister.
But the fire had cooled.
His wound wouldn't cauterize.
Like a man bleeding to death from a scratch,
he would perish from a single scorching, burning event:
a hemophilia of tragedy.

And in the aftermath,
the ash blew on the wind
and through the cornfields
like leaflets and pamphlets
proposing anonymous tranquility
as I lay unconscious on the floor of the engine-room, a prophet remembering.

III.

Terrible time it was mixing into that solvent earth;
we had spent night after night digging at the soil
trying to raise something above our heads in a ringing cry,
and there were only nettles mixed in . . . that's all we found.

Raking leaves we toiled month after month,
and nothing—nothing.
We went into town and saw
a heroin motorcade move past,
letting bags of white celebrity
fall from the cracks
in their limousine windows.

The streets were filled with wild and frantic people
hoping to get a glimpse behind murky windows,
a glimpse of something—something
round and soft that we could take to the salted fields with us,
something like a balm—found in
brilliant little concave groves
weary in their threadbare simplicity—
to soothe our yellow and bloody hands.
We followed the procession of limousines
out of town as if they were pipers
dressed in reflecting black.

We followed until we were all standing
at the doors of our trailers breathing heavily
the perfumed exhaust and musk of the earth.
We stood solemnly watching as the last limousine
disappeared behind our local smithy's forge,
tempering cocaine dreams with our calloused foreheads.

The fields were fertile with stone and ash
when we returned to them that night.
A boy, with dirt already creased in the folds
of his skin, came to us as we walked home.

Awe made a radio of his face as he said,
"I found this stone in the earth today. . . .
It glitters."

Years later concrete had replaced a hazy carpet.
A parking lot was laid over our red land
and we longed for shoes. There weren't many left.
Most had moved on, but we would kneel as the sun rose

and chant the only words we had left,
"I found this stone in the earth today. . . .
It glitters.
I found this stone in the earth today,
I found this stone in the earth today,
it glitters, it glitters."

IV.

The train was picking up speed toward Promontory;
and the last glittering spike—dislodged by some thrill seeker,
some treasure hunter in the midnight of our generation's nightmare war—
offered up its great weight to our onrushing, unattended locomotive.
One-Eye had just detached the cars for speed,
was just about to bind my unconscious soul
hand and foot for a later use, when the cattle scoop struck gold—
struck, only to continue its direction, now hurtling end-over-end, into the center of town.
I was brought to by the force of our landing, and in that instant of chaos and blood
and fire, I saw. It was no Saul road, nor fiery weed,
but it was an enemy, and it was not of this Earth.
I saw.

Picking my broken and wracked body off the floor,
I exited the train
to see One-Eye lifting himself from the dirt
in front of the Sheriff's Office, having been thrown clear
of the spinning locomotive and the coal.
There was no shoot-out, no high drama
in the streets of Promontory, no Morricone drawl in the background—
my Oregon, my Elysian fields, my *Paradise Regained*,
was now impossible. Not for the bill, the warrant
and its differing values for capture or decapitation,
but for that terrible vision, that great lie we called our Savior.
Instead, there was a clean, point-blank bullet hole
in his face, right between what used to be his eyes.

I don't remember much after I pulled the trigger for the first time,
but when they finally wrapped me in adamantine cuffs around both arms and legs,
my gun swallowed into my Being;
after they dragged me away,
throwing the key into the Marianas Trench;
after that show trial, that juridical circus,
I was told the charge: wholesale slaughter of innocents:
women, children, men, dogs, cows, horses (I suppose they caught me
gnawing on some weeds—I'd already burned everything that would . . .),
and destruction of a national treasure:

that stone tie, or at least what they think is that authentic golden spike, now on display
in a new exhibit at the Smithsonian commemorating the dying and dead frontier,
while I await my own kind of tourists behind as much plate and steel
as the Declaration.

V.

I have become nothing more than the nameplate on the door outside
this room. The paths of sweat running down these walls,
interrupted by scratched messages left there
by the generations interred as I am now,
are defined merely by their return to the metal grating that collects
all fluids in one drain in the center of the floor.
Having gotten to a certain point, there was no further land to traverse, no boundaries to
            cross:
the rails led straight here as they twisted across the great expanse of land behind.
I was taken out of my sleeper and directed from the platform to here,
to this room with its one window overlooking the water, bay, and city.

My keepers wear nothing but white frocks occasionally stained by blood and shit;
they told me this was a kind of cure, a way to find myself
under the great cloudy sphere above; I was told I would need nothing else.

At night, when my keepers go home to their prefab homes on the shore,
I read the messages that cost fingernails and time,
the words that cover every inch of these walls—I read for a few hours
then sleep. My one amenity is a coffee maker and it keeps me up sometimes with its
            gurgling and sputtering
and the darkness it spreads. I am leaving this account here
like all the accounts surrounding me, to give you who will come after again and again some
            testimony of the pushes' end that is now
falling back into the sea of wheat and the plains that once seemed endless.
I am leaving this message to affirm the promise made to me of a plot of land—
this is it. Nothing has been denied me, everything came through eventually.
I hardly need to say that it was all I had ever hoped for and more.
Could I ever have imagined a number so great that is the infinity of this room?

If you are here, you might want to look under the mattress.
I have left there that last golden spike, that last mineral piece of stone
my train dislodged on its crescendo of a run and that came careening,

but the little of it we had pieced together[16]
painted her with a viciousness, a grandiosity of violence
that would better befit one with a different moniker.[17]
For now, we simply called her Stranger.

Reborn in this late century, her pure unaltered DNA,
her original limbs and organs, her unadulterated metabolism still
appropriate to this dimming planet made her vital
to the cause. And though she would not thaw out
for a while still, we had smuggled her out of the tower,
the bastion of our contact with the heavens.

A stranger in a strange land corrupted—
falsified by our will to dominate landscape: nothing.
For some reason we thought she gave us a chance,
a fighting chance against this terrible paralysis, this post-apocalyptic
fury that had been unleashed, this complete control exercised
from above, from without, from within—

she still had the Colt .45 holstered to her belt,

---

as if fated, into my right hand before I disembarked.
I have written a name on the bottom: the name of the last to come
and the grave that now holds what you should be looking for.
Memorize this name and destroy the spike if you can.
Many would die for much less knowledge of it, but you, my eventual roommate
in this hotel of wearied presence, I gift to you the last piece
of the puzzle that might finally fit into the keyhole
and open the door on this last piece of untouched land.
Why, you ask, are you worthy of this information? Why, you ask,
is there an answer to all of it?
Because there is nothing left. Because you are *here*,
right where you should be, and for now will remain here
until you can decode the messages that lie beside this one.
This makes you worthy. Not because you have traveled across that tightrope stretched
between New York and Los Angeles,
but because there is no rope, and no poles with which to climb to the height
of what was never there in the first place.
I hope you have found this useful. The keepers are about to slide my bread and water
through the tiny slit in the door, so I will return,
always and forever, return to this and other messages, later.
I hope you suffer this room better than I have.
They are comi—

[end transmission]
[16] Also see Appendix I.
[17] Saint of Killers.

its legendary call-and-response something not heard
for millennia—myth come back from the envy
of men and the imagination of women.
The capacity for passionate violence still
resided in her muscle-corded limbs.

Ours was lost in the sea of contemporary purges.

Horus and Anubis had descended,
unleashed upon our comrades as well as our leaders.
There was nothing to be done. We had to summon her.
She was the only thing that could set things aright.

The aquamarine web laid quickly fifty-or-so meters from the tower
was our only hope of survival.

ii.

On the ancient highway to Phoenix, pocked and straddled with boards,
our vehicle hit a bump and overturned itself. She would be thawed too
        soon!
And open fire she did. Nothing could stop her terrestrial judgment.
As if all the horrors of a life lived, from one point of fidelity to the next,
the immanent changes and the gradual becomings into new seats of fire—
her awakening was so . . . organic. Like a journey where one starts

in frame one, a man sitting at a bar, smoking a cigarette, a little bit drunk
but none worse for the wear, through adventures that necessarily
        culminate
in the awakening and finding of powers, the recession of them, the
        discovery of new ones,
until the man is fighting gods themselves, defeating them, rising,
        awakening again,
promoting himself into higher and higher universes where ultimate
        nirvana,
true enlightened bliss enters, fought for, but strangely destined with what
        combination
of free will there may exist, until the story ends, last panel, with the self-
        same man
sitting at a bar, smoking a cigarette, a little bit drunk but none worse for
        the wear,

fade to credits, gallery of stills, written and drawn by: []¹⁸—she glared at
    our hollowed-out eyes
and replacement epidermis, our transplanted brains and reconstructed
    heads, and with no matter of compunction,
shattered our every existence with bullets from before immortality.
The gods—Isis, Osiris, all the rest—could not help but to fall to this
    Saint of Killers, this hate born to rule, and to judge, and to
    replace.

---

[18] Bardo Lièr Parté.

B. Two Parts of a Parallax Gap[19]

i. After the Dance

Extreme:	Extreme:	Extreme:
Desert.	Ocean.	Desert.
[20]	[21]	[22]

(*The Universe Had to reConstruct Itself Out of the Most Available Elements, and New Physical Laws Had to be Instituted to Prevent singular unity, originary or not.*)

Observation of all subjects had to cease and our authorship was compr(om)ised.[23, i] It was a [time] that form could only coalesce into broken and fragmented train tracks. We[24] were known to rest comfortably sipping drinks on the edge of that galactic deep; we continued to tell ourselves not to access faith in a Great Narrator. The background music made this difficult. Stereo- had given way to mono-phonics.[25]

Perceiving a train traveling south through the mountains was the only chanting lyric accompanying this primeval scene contained in the ash of cigarettes. This had to be the work of the pure multiple. The work of collecting some sets together.

Could we feel a beginning? Was it like reading someone else's children poetry?[26] And yet some things were about to coalesce. . . .

There were various sections, myths, and anthologies seemingly springing from an oceanic depth.[j] There, where consciousness[27] and its leapings were absconding

---

[19] Galactic Being and Prisoner of Alcatraz
[20] H
[21] O
[22] H
[23] Of a small library, an old teletype-laptop, and as many augmentations, legal or otherwise, as were available.
[24] Who had come to be known by a name familiar in the penny-dreadfuls: The Watchers.
[25] Propagated by rhizomatic vision.
[26] We are not in a position to answer these questions, we are only able to tell you what we know of this [time], and we must delve deep into the hyperarchive to accomplish this. Things have gotten a little confused.

by the [infinite-minute], we observed. Eight things
were defining their own utterances against this background,
eight moments from that deepness in the sky.[28] (Or was it seven. . . ?)

After the dance, the party was the thing, what
could suffer attachments, entrances and exits, and
it was rumored to be *fun*. Things were happening.
Yes, we all agreed as we sauntered around the punchbowl,
"some*thing* had gone horribly wrong." Conferring,
we realized there was nothing to be done, not even to wait.
But the horizon was beginning to define itself;
we were mistaken into thinking this illusory-temporal-boundedness
was something like an investigation. It wasn't a problem
that we were wrong, and that this misreading created
voices. It was enough to inhabit an interval, a gap
between this and that, between this recombinant theater
and a **Conversation Among the Ruins**.[k]

---

[27] Not yet committed to phenomenological entertainments, epistemic violence, or pataphysical, retrograde retribution, the stars, see, they looked like stations on this flow chart of becoming, places we could see some about to arrive and depart for destinations unknown, even to archival outflowing itself. Could we sense what was gathering? Not really, but there was a singular voice coming across what might be called the highlands, something along the lines of individuation and experiential discourse . . . something like an "I." Something, however, not laced with what had gone before, but coming out of the void left by the story we had observed.

[28] Deep logic, deep interface, deep connections, deep structure. There was a fire upon the deep and there were some diving into orthographematics.

ii. The[29] Apocalypse Archive

It is the narrator's task to . . . charged by . . . to watch. . . .
No, there is simply an endnote of collection.[1]
No, not even that.[m] Why, asked tomorrow,
the invocation? There is still quite a bit here.
Isn't there? (So much pessimism. . . .[30])

We can grant a few things as approaching veracity:

1) The circuits of the archive are analogous to what appear
as threads of a tapestry. 2) The tapestry is not complete.
3) The tapestry belies incompleteness.[31] 4) *It* is not a "tapestry"
at all. 5) Each thread can be collected, though not
in a mode of frayed-edge destruction.[32] 6) "Two" threads
symbolize railroad tracks. 7) Others do not. 8) Beginning
with these, raveling and unraveling will occur. 9) We collect
these threads. 10) We have no use for these threads.
11) The fabric is one of melting. 12) The circuits do not
resemble a tapestry. 13) Totalization cannot be expressed
as will. 14) Circuitry is another way of saying "landscape."
15) Desire is ambiguous here. 16) The hyperarchive is
an expression of the end. 17) The hyperarchive is an expression
of *a* beginning. 18) The hyperarchive is never
aware of itself, is always aware of itself, is found in nature.

---

[29] . . . Always Incomplete . . .
[30] The prison house of the dictionary.
[31] And standing reserve.
[32] (What was the tale again? Did the hero triumph?)
We were set to watch but have now become involved.
What we have observed will not follow but traverses
the sea bed. There is nothing to do but catalog.
And we would like to introduce someone. He may
(or may not) have anything to communicate, but he
cannot help but intrude between stations—a conductor
(if you will) with buttons to signal the "all aboard!"
With each oscillation between himself
and us (and others), another entry is deleted from this log.

To introduce a voice over the loudspeaker during intermission
as a brief rendezvous in the yard was not our intended way
of indicating that this is all part of a cover-up, that, in fact,
the jig was up long ago, that we are merely collecting the fragments
of the end, that we are all eschatologists, tenured, fat, and happy
while we do favors for cartons of cigarettes and write a certain horizon's
eulogy. We need no intention when it comes to the perfectly obvious.

19) What follows subjects itself to whatever can be aforesaid.
20) Someone[33] was wrong. 21) Things have no place here.
22) The desert is growing more palpable everyday;
vision is desired but avoidance culpable—do not judge.
23) Diabolism is a manner of coping with the ocean.
24) Transgression cannot be symptomatic if not liminal.
25) Totality and fragmentation copulate into the evening
until circuitry dissolves and we are bathed in water
for watching what has taken place and what is avoided:
the accumulating dread and joy of unfolding and veiling,
what is and is not revealed by curtailment and outflowing.[34, 35]

---

[33] Pythagoras.
[34] This rocking chair.
[35] Mere collection cannot exist in a narrative mode.

III.

A. Three Months, the Ship Is Waiting

        Summer's castaway length   stripped bare the ship
        piled in corner   labels and oscillating names
                                                      blank beds stacked against the
                                                       wall

        space enough
        for the price of water
        and what postcards

I wish it hadn't gone like this, hadn't looped its serpent head into the grass-green escape, hadn't followed paths of slick jelly fantasy. I wish the damn menagerie would have stayed steely in place, behind the carousel, away from the camera lens. Months stagger forward. A pendulum swing and ride telling the cabbie two revolving and contradictory stories, which would have sucked the paper out of this whole thing, this year bent into cul-de-sacs. I cannot remember when the overseer left or when the company drowned all its officers in the lake. Singled out, I was told to walk, to escape along these paths. As was everyone else. There was just not enough left to sell. It wasn't cowardice. Just too many hambone fiddles and crockery and wasted lies.

        Summer's lasting jubilee   a conquest, a signet ring
        stamp on this wax   blinded eye over a labyrinth
        and drums
        tilted panels
        shot through
        with wine
                                            a foxgun pointed like lipstick
                                            the selling point meters down
                                            from waiting crash sites
                                            of windup hornets and birds
        call   there are listeners   if not here

        melody and some grains
        that refused sifting
                                            an easy tongue bath
                                            despite rough skin

        the plane arrived
        despite the rain
                                            and sweat-heat dominated
                                            until sleep took over

clack clack keys lost coffin buried old postmortem
                        and sleeping there judging locks subterraneous
noon wish stranger smile instantaneous click
                        mixed catalytic converter drink in warehouse
whereby parts designated auto fall into cardboard
                        destined for miasma new after the drive
but capricious trucker swallowed whole
                        and thus midnight all over screaming
oh my fucking god

Last week waiting for the bus, after I'd finally gotten out, gotten out of the whole thing, I was startled as a parachute fluttered down to rest a few feet away, minus jumper. Pure chance? And the chance that I had so much money seemed to dictate that I wrap the briefcase holding it all in the parachute and leave it for whomever might stumble across this keen little alleyway. It didn't matter anymore. I was out. Of course, $203,000 was a lot of cash to carry. But in those days, I usually had at least $50,000 in my pocket, primarily to satisfy the whims of band members who might venture out for a spontaneous shopping spree. Jimmy often purchased antiques when we were in America and he always found it easier to negotiate a good deal if he could put cash on the table.[n]

Summer's diamond and sapphire needles
                        rending through the chronology of Strauss
toward metamorphosis, yet collared early
                        in the mixing of phlebotomy's product

revolving now Babel cry the buildings	past dry riverbed
piece by piece and columns	mosaics falling the roof pocked and fading no urns but beyond
Greek or otherwise a city and fortress hurricane sky heat sensed infrared was sweat coalescence of yet *Naqoyqatsi* hanging in the air	spinning on a new axis the palette foam and desire vision transcendent war and brides of numbers smelling of hypertext protocol

The rally was mistaken for a rock concert. Midway through, after screaming for two hours, the music stopped and one sentence was uttered: "Khrushchev and Salinger were better picks in their own way."[o] And then only the sound of a dot matrix printer scrawling out the names of everyone's ancestors could be heard over the loudspeaker. Fifteen bottles backstage. Waiting like harvest nights, row upon row upon row of photo negatives, easy smoke, and pumping derricks. T-shirts were sold. The outline of a double-necked guitar carried by the drum major's silhouette drawn on. Confusion was the military band marching in to stake their claim in the middle of the Exchange. Against the wall were slot machines. Hands. And a train running over these tracks.

summer's midway nostalgia	stilted spinning
Challenger's last piece	echotube child
	floating above
a certain kindness	Jupiter swallowing itself
	the names
grid projection	sidled along *Glas*
territories phantoms	circuit conductivity
row upon row	handbooks for such
and appliances	the pope was lost
in the aisles	thanks

clickety somewhere waxwork faces in retrograde
                      dumpster clinic's *oeuvre* of falling walls
taking flight and mixed sight and bullets
                      and Gorbachev sentence in language brief
this was the lucky drainage-tube of radiation
                      passing the day success sugar taxes
catatonic down time or screaming again
                      oh my fucking god

The trolley car was filled. Dangling off the side. To the pictures. Boy next to me. Whispering. Could only make out a few words. "Need concrete guidelines   'special character'   universality of the concept of being. For we may   being by way of special interpretation of a particular being: Led Zeppelin, in which the horizon for an understanding and a possible interpretation of being is to be won. But   'historic,' so that proper   ontological   illumination   necessarily becomes a[n]   interpretation."[p] Got off at the next stop.

Always do. Like the walk past the capitol building. Showings pretty slim pickings. Guess I'll go see *Concord* for the eighth time.[36, 37]

summer's footnoted end	circle takes the square
battleground civil and immediate	light from behind
going from start	infinity a home
across the way	smokestacks and reactors
three miles	an island
	building's façade
approach not	door's will opens
staring only a mirror	
teach it	express lane
winding through	a walk would be kinder

---

[36] *Concord*, dir. Hans Milton (Pittsburgh, PA: Zimmerman Pictures Ltd., 1935). The film enjoyed a brief but overwhelming critical success. It has been completely lost to time in a fire that also deleted all the work of Milton. Arson suspected. It was said that this was Brando's first role, a nine year old, but reports cannot be confirmed since the film has ceased to exist and Brando would not (and did not) comment. Like the controversy over Shakespeare's authorship, it will never be resolved for the conspiracy-head.

[37]

Summer's evening walk	stamp quiet posture
nuns in evening gowns	prowling organ streets
pipes to ceiling	back down again
	the marks on the page history
fit together excerpt	footnote the footnote
understanding a long line	at the shelter
bread a penny	boil that sweet cabbage
read the lines	something there
	life resembles
not horizontal	vertical blinds
capture moments	crying relief
rather substance	spilling coffee
watching the paths	it might take
away away	and toward

It would have been nice, I suppose, to let that summer lie—lie reposed and unconcerned. The caves my parents took me to were covered in figures of humans hunting animals. It was a long trip, difficult to see Cape Canaveral a few days later. Everything was increasing and decreasing intervals. Arpeggios of meaning. It would have been nice to listen to one sound for days, one note ringing and ringing and ringing. Highway 101 down the Oregon Coast found us at each other's throat. Headphones *an* answer. The Grand Canyon was obscured by snow and fog and mist. A great abyss of white and gray. Standing at the edge—always fixing to do something about it down there, or up here, for that matter—standing there, the tightrope I saw stretching across (and no one else) was too thin and I would fall. Instead, I built track long enough to reach across and laid it over that gaping hole. And it would be nice to say that this is that track. I've given it the right form, but there are still the holes. If I could paint, I would fill them all in the starkest black, but the shadows on the backs of my eyelids are unfocused, and the patterns too complicated to reproduce. So, with nothing else, here I am.

imposition yes
apology at the bottom   the lake not yet dry
yet step back   look, vision
Saul piecemeal   phenomenal inquiry
was origin   and imperative
took to basement   and there
found presence   emitting hierarchically
yet row upon row   collapsing houses

Summer's joining with seasons
like hands stretched between buildings
read the cost of being stranded
as fortuitous fire burning
the last pages for warmth
against postcards sent
but forgotten in the movement,
the revision of all themes
destined to fall from the trees
and hit the ground and sink in.
Summer's castaway end
was a ship sent from distant harbors
to ferry it home, to ferry it back;
and summer's expectance
was to lie in beds of saturated becoming
while the months rolled over the tracks
in an eternal loop.

B.i. Effluvium

Hall of ambient moorings,

       this quietude, this stillness . . .
not merely a looking over my shoulder to see (an)other
languid tiding(s) flush with ropes and striated patterns of sand moving the
       snake soft belly of these beaches forward,
not simply the gamut of brain cells responding to the drone of parasitic
       and flea bitten corsairs ready to wake the downgrade toil of
       waves,
not found shaped patterns rising headlong into a practice above the
       distant herculean effort of pitch-forth,
but the moldy wobble of the peach pit coming to rest in its origin of
       future and void:

n., *pl.*—via or –vi-ums [L, a flowing out, outlet] 1) a real or supposed
       outflow in the form of a vapor or stream of invisible particles;
       aura—
I was there on the platform to see a woman disembark who I was not
       waiting for, nor was she expecting me, but there she was, looking
       everywhere for whomever was supposed to meet her.
2) a disagreeable or noxious vapor or odor—
the train disembarked belching steam and hissing its screech of memory.

What once fed me, what once cradled my empirical self in the basket of
       nutritional ecstasy
has, of course, vanished.
Not to worry. There are still plenty of pianos in the world.
Da   da   da   da,   dadadum.[38]

The marmoset calm files past like a transgression of some cotton
       boundary: the libidinal croquet separating myself from my lungs.
       Mornings
I wake half-past these watered-down rites of disenfranchised
       horticulturalists, greeting the dance with a wave and a smile.
       There are three things:
1) Our personal hallucination now develops as boundlessly as perhaps the
       total nightmare of human society, for instance . . . 2) readiness
       from now on to be the survivor of some great impending tragedy

---

[38] *Dasein.*

is a must 3) abandon the farm and head to Arizona where it's warm.

Four more things: 1) the sky is as brightly occluded as 2) the festoons dropped from on high by wavering 3) calliopes in the 4) midnight garden again.

A butcheress stands at the end of my hall, waving her huge porcelain-skinned knife. I say hello.

The time has come to pay attention to the limits I have drawn around myself with coalchalk. (Mr. Leone might agree . . . and then again, he might not.)

Come take me. Time is short and I've spent far too long hoisting the gables around, trying their soon to be ivy task with a whittling perfection.

Come let the dogs out of their kennel. They have mussed enough of the newspaper laid down. Give them new ground.

The four-hearted men and women share a similar destiny with those who have none.

(If only vision were merely a word. If only cataracts were as easy to fit and take off as contact lenses.)

Come sink the double-down in slippery waves of traffic off the turnpike in marshy Lafayette. There are stores there where one has to wait, like in a doctor's office, for anything. They don't call your name but rather gesture in symbols and bark out code, and everyone knows this, except for me, who is stuck in traffic.

I have said it before but now I am positively sure that I really mean it: I am ready for the *heart-skip-beat-mambo*.

Not like when I used to walk on concrete that would melt the rubber of my soles, not like smoky cafes, all wooden and pale, not the real meaning anymore—the implied importance—but the actual act, and yet I wonder how to start.

Occult and psychic phenomenon, pollution, stench, exhalation: Kirlian photography, glossolalia, Ouija® (bo-ard[/-red]), exteriorized protoplasm, biofeedback, sink into miasma new after the game, the tournament of willful and willing souls all hung up by their fingernails—

Effluvium—come round up the spring hikers, with their matching orange backpacks, with their sunglasses and locked briefcases—there are dangerous things in those woods.

How, above all other things, did digital delay get to the point that it

is the most sonorous of all effects, of all music?
And again, I find it odd to read about things I can tell you about: the desert of the real, I grew up there . . . I've just been misplaced by practicality or something that resembles it.
My favorite part of a glass of water is the little, almost invisible shards of ice waiting to melt at the bottom.
I hope everything is going well and the posts that you are anchored to are becoming a little more circumscribed, sincerely.

ii. A Second E(ff)luvium

The mild vibrations are clocking in at about one-tenth their supposed weight: the bird's nest falling in the absence of gravity; so gesture through, young house-painter, the transgression is closer at hand than your simple categorical leave-taking of haunted limbs. Your every move resounds in the walls, falling through pinafore masks—silhouettes with no corresponding reference: clowns, clowns, clowns, clowns, clowns to excommunicate now dull edged grins. Order=trip the fright fantastic as you go through the spinning jenny, an abysmally loud nightmare of folding ebullience. Everything is going to be just awful. Trust the mistakes to the shakers, they might say, pleased to meet you, show me the world. Young man, there needs to be more teal in the overhang—not the vulture black and carry-on blues, but rather mixed support beams goldentriangulated through the back door of harried (oh the endless fields). Under dying suns there are only a few left wrappers that once contained such rubber delights as only you might disapprove of, you now taking a smoke break by the pool and not even paying attention. Work makes you harderbiggerfasterlighter, more a nexus, more a realization that powerwork is neverover. The dictionary is open to its nine-hundred ninety-ninth page. Can you read what it says there, near the top? Octillion, yes. One followed by twenty-seven zeros. The world is not waiting on you. There must be a distance between you and it, yes, but it does not wait. You once were welcomed to what some would call the desert of the real, but you shook your lanky body, informing everyone that you grew up there. There is no sistinic drive here, just color and form, not even colorfield, but a job to cover over the old holes made by nails in the wall.

Falling between one dilemma and another, the rise and fall of humanistic debate ravaging time immemorial that is a certain index of petty tragedies, a solvency of misappropriation designating the half-consumed litter clogging the alleys of iron-bound passion-fruit—next time do not let the codex, the list of names, follow the dramatic urges that spurn one on toward the piracy of time-pieces. Designate the power broker on the shopping mall lawn with blue. To designate is to follow the cramps now forming in legs and arms, soon to be realized, of course, and disavowing any specific relationship between the ravages of space and the celestialism, nigh taciturn compulsion, of speculation: the party at the end of the superimposed gigantosphere. This is where the bus stops if it had not been so clogged with people. Mix the quality of desideratum pale-light and up-bring the phosphorescence. Big green jelly ape, there are mixtures of turning crazy lunatic birth, engenderments of commonality below the tree-line philistine. Do not let the voice of the people come to rest underneath the circumnavigation of talismaniacs/voodoo-mobsters. Yon! There are new divulgences, new transgressions to make-up-the-breakdown. Dissociation begets the farm implement/hand disaster of the new spring hallucination in the coma soft down philandered all around the nonsense. Read this as you will, for there is truly nothing to be done with it other than wander and pour, as if into a glass (though there may be something in it already, surely not bile) and then reconfigure by situating the whole thing to simply color and deregulation: this is *a* desire, but there isn't necessarily something seeping out the chrome functionality that *should* be the contested aberration, the fought over nix on the bell. Pull the octopus through the Plantagenet whole. Then there will be hole new limits of systematically questioning the other powder bits, the other seeds that work as if from below cerulean measure, but why is it always the direction that . . . and it brings up questions of . . . course it does, and then this would be how one would speak all the time, not as if there were some hoped for canon with specific direction, but rather nothing simply at all except fastidious traipsing over the never-ground. Communicate. Listen fair sir, there are only a few things left to be untried by the categorical imperative monster devouring itself while holding it all together. Let us not be worried about the fantastic conundrum at the heart of this entire race towards global distraction, it is right t/(everyw)/here—dastardly commandos of language, who would attack and only exist so as to train for more assassination—this is not desired of the desire movement that we have now all signed on for and let focus our energy so vibrantly as to become overcome with the trepidation that consumes even the most fervent of analysts in the new democratic discovery of pain and jubilation, except, what harbors new and wholly transfixed realities is neither camouflage nor dirt; yon figure of repose, I congratulate you on seeing one most worthy; thy exquisite pain divulges toward the all and yet has a clear focus of the gray when the window is open. Focus! Mitosis is coming a full click earlier than it was going to, with a head of steam; dragnets are being spread through every trash collection to find the culprit who started the dignity wars; on pain of death there are street-sweeps who gnash teeth for a morsel of flatlander bread; it is a one-dimension shenanigan, a dumb-show put on for the clearest, most malignant tumor growing pus ball staring at bare breast and bone—the fever is but a ruse to drum up support for the beautiful and the sublime. Romantics are drunks on clever boats, smart apes with nothing to do but stare the self-same prophecy in the mirror of sense while hooting and hollering at the witch-crawling sympathy. Devil, out with you! There are far too many things that go unnoticed on the envy ship: not the fools but the prison, not the patient but the cure—these are the call-to-arms-actions [block in the head of syndrome] foregrounding of the system mixture tenaciously;

Felix says, oh look at the stars, and he was right. Not just right in the fallen sense of the word, but the texting of the microphone right that dittoes the camera new. Fine. For what mere symbols could hope to—save him, save her, save them, save it—save that thing over there starving against the wall, save it a few . . . wait! Did you hear that? They must be coming; up the gangplanks and raise anchor, there are pirates to skewer! This is not an easy drumming into the backside of love affairs. No, something else entirely, the hogwash Miss of the award show dinner. Yes. So much inside that needs to come pouring out, but too much, so that there is a huge artery blocked with lymphomaniacality; worse, the mob of blockage is creeping corpuscular limbs—forward the chant goes, and all stops with the realization that one could go forever and never really say anything amidst the howls and screeching of those who would never be with mountains nor camels to trek up them, and yet below, below there is this overwhelming feeling of inebriation that never truly got started and surely has not ended the hopes of the simple-minded middle folk one would pander to if they could grouse up the affectation and respect to soil oneself in the crystal milk-bath holy waters of everything and everyone; but no, these are not the times for that. The space will never open up; the ground will never be found. For an informed look at the state of things we now turn to our correspondent in the field who will introduce the warbling of the pigeon bone arrows that have come piercing through the windows this lovely autumn evening only to fix a hole in our wall so big that we must get someone to repair it immediately, otherwisethebirdsmightflyrightinandwesurelydon'twantthatnowdowe?Imeandowe!?

IV.

Through the dirigible scansion of frittered nomenclature,
arias of Texas-leaguers whittled down to a few crass markings (numbers
     inflated with meaning),
the dilettante's brush with scattered folios and eccentricities of crowded
     aural copulation,
introduction of forward thinking prefaces into the table with burning
     cinders of asterisks and hieroglyphics,
parcel-post to the quick-drying lands,

fold half-hands and linger
body. Heed illuminating spheres.
Suppose waiting and patience were inseparable amnesiacs,
fitted during manufacture, fit for kings and all else too—
forlorn drippings of tongues, in part a hollowness.

Nein fragments. Nix cutlass strokes of thought.
Hatteras clunking down the stairs of stumbling concision.
"For the only tears to have gamb(o)led upon the page
were staunch recipients of their own grafted demiurgy,"
quoth the long-standing publican in the night-flowing drapery,
orange cowl wrapped around steadfast wings of hourglass ice
and golden skin. [Fie!] The quickening is about to begin
as we lapse to trace through that device into subaltern realms,
mixing our own fear upon meeting Tamex the False Metal.
The glowing red abyss abounding about your bound soul creeps
slowly through the waxen yule logs, yet the borderland mysteries,
the misty air of desert towns forgetting themselves in the harbor of their
     own salvation. . . .
Seated there, in your imagined stool, hundreds of hat-racks and a sullen
     gnome,
can you not see that you have stumbled into the Real? "Can you not,"
as the saying goes, "see the forest for the great yawning nothing
     surrounding you?"
This fight or flight mode does not become you. There isn't enough
     motion,
not enough inducement of the humors that are so necessary to your
     curious little kind.
[Woe.] There is much to terrify those who would attempt a history,
     those
whose minds set your burred little feet to wandering for their own
     devices.

Stop-gap the chrysanthemums in holy ways rather than mix-out this devil-boredom,
the truly engendering path of those other, taller folk—this square payment
forged in the clasps of our own will-locks handed down as we descend, forcing, nay,
not only our knowledge of ultimate undoing, but all you can see around you at this moment.
Little one, what is to be your fate on this ill-begotten eve in the Abyss?[39]

---

[39] I am not so sure it has nothing to do with rounding the bases. . . .

A. Meditations on the Diabolic

i. Prelude for the Devil

Not in the manner in which ideology is represented, so much so that *ideology* is *represented*.

"Focus" is a large word. The destitution example is always that of strange agrarians.

Manifestation, again, enacts itself in language as if the consumptive arrangement of wordy smiths consume the overlain factors of the democratization figures like so many clear complete hegemonies of alternate culture—ensue.

A mythopraxis traces difference as if the overlain proximities trust the almagest—censure the appropriate manifestation of the Satan Trismagest. Altogether now . . . in sequence of what adumbrates the filial attachments with which we photograph our own insecurities, our own hopeful misappropriations of the secret manifest; oh woe, the things that conspire against the hopeful acceptance, nihil, moxotopianism, lord don't let the symptomatic brood in the infernal copulation of the easement of transient—oh so easy to criticize, but to understand—and not even as if there were any hope of the former resting in the all encompassing of the banal lucidity—mythopraxis and difference play in the ultimate. . . .

ii. For the Infernal Pit Shall Never Hold Celestial Spirits in Bondage

There is a way in which *they* can be ended.
Be on alert
                for no performance necessary:

dust clinging the night-sill against arpeggios
of descent, trees of pestilential pride
hanging thin boughs toward the sway
of craven wooly-word, epigones
bringing desert-lash to bear upon landscape. . . .

This, the middle-way
to the end of a closet
(middle part sliding over lower door),
where hanging a miserly foot over foundation:
the measurement of a nutshell.
Corresponding to a perimeter north
and south found in Thallophytes
eating stomachs of bread not made—nothing
to stick in esophagus or for rolling tongues
across quarter-knuckles, knives of asyndenton—
chariot-land-mines are clutched
in Mammon's hands while he,
iterating some possibility of attaining
previous grace—
still a slavery.

iii. *Die Götterdämmerung, oder, den Spiegel vorhalten?*

Left were two men on the summit of our present time—a finis for the
    Bruhnhilde who was to become eunuch, interred by frostbite
mit keinem Schließer—; one was to set out despite what was to be eventually
    held up to her: his long ago buried phallus as a monument to the
    cockeyed and razed landscape from which they sprang, a mention
    terrible in the night-moment of indeterminacy.
The other, a sexy Siegfried with buttocks abrogating in a last gasp, a
    pedigree of normative stances, was to starve hysterical at
    crossroads in the wake of twilight and reflection
from the mirror that stood stoically while *tu marches sur des morts* toward the
    fugue of C minor, which must be sped up if accommodating
    expunged *Weltschmerz* could ever hold as its monkish position a
    classic of dried parchment up to the light, *oder schaufen, oder
    laufen*—away, away and toward.
The crime committed was simply designated power and domination. And
    if the two stared into the icy heat of their mountain, there was to
    be a testament of static in the participation and adoration of grisly
    moment.

What was picked in-halted canopy (but forgotten? the stars?) that left
    hemophiliacs of these but two yeomen crowded under sunny
    pipal tree with voices risen from unearthed revolvers excavated
    from this plain, this ghost town? Next to the iron
of one was found spectacles and a schedule . . . and a pendulum that
    would sway with the sun if hung above certain ox-white
    gloaming; what was to become of this landslide, this photo-album
    of labels, this sound that slays us young, this fortnight of *das frühe
    Mittelalter?*
Cymbals of palms crash.

iv. Definitely Not Advice. It Comes from the Divel, the True Master and Giver of Such Rapture

. . . am vulture tired of giving directions,
of scavenging any opinion whatsoever
[whomever these bits of strangers belong to]—
not by half the lucky consumption of classically regrown liver,
not by far the tearing of one's own eyes,
but the silent refuse picked off this material project,
this bulimic harbor-entrance of empirical crowded hallways
ending in a gnawed gateway where to spit a few droplets
through a rusted keyhole [a pink-eyed entrance
to a slow, flabby understanding] would be tantamount to
bee-sized flash droplets of a trembling glance
arriving at what is, as through a glass—
in the pleasures of bed, hermeneutics of books,
and forging them in a certain fire of loathing
for the manner in which to be taken
from the palsied eye of those who would listen
to the crenellated word-fortress of the I am),
an easement of intent and tone must couple
with the gentle sway of letting be
if ever soft sleep is to be offered, still alive.

(And here I am, at it again.
It would be better and easier
to write technical manuals, instructing
how to break the yule-mask, stream the perfect image
of the perfect parallel we make with the wall at home
while following the line all the way down to
watch the night space of this dreaming.)
You would see. We shook.

v. A Statue of the Destroyer Lies Beneath Layers of Salt

Dead Sea indigo net catches damask inkblots of increasing buoyancy.
Floating powerless, the goatherd misses the grand entrance of one liar.
Jezebel, where does the taxi-auto stop in the colorform space of waiting?
Surely not underneath ahabitation's waiting spear, or call me an extreme
        case
of iseikonia—Jerusalem Cherries, the eyes purport one large sackcloth
        dream—
the point that is filled in, mostly drowned in this condition of seeing one
burning. Rite of indeterminate identity slowing dull ragged in the bone
hollow of nettle last—for years. Banebridge, you slightly occluded
        coming,
the ferry boat over this wracked water,

                    missile the overture tonight—where
are the Templars feeding on drum and silver trombone, golden coronet
misty play of slight young people carrying weapons much too large,
        weapons of fallen angels?—carry Pentateuch-salves away
            on that once silent road to Damascus, the færie
                mother motions neglected, rout the boar
                    and begin that clarineted ritual
                        the summer before the lord
                            of locusts consumes
                                buzzing
                        and the stopwatch set
for the grand architecture of catalepsy. Incantation, relax, it is trapped in
        stone.

vi. The Code Is Just as Unwieldy Upside Down

Four-hundred years ago we saw the Acropolis still devastated ruins
littering the junk-bed wavering of the splinter-wedged gap
of parcel and post by water and air. Time 7:34now—make it a great day—
airline stocks are actually rallying a bit this morning. . . .

Your organs stretched on the Turing Machine and the trace is not
haptic. Time is breaking the eggshell of three vocal soarings.
One punch in the ribs to set those beautiful arms swinging in a dance of
        names.
I will release myself!contract out on the new bestiary tonic

spas in that sad little desert, that myth making breakdown of sun
and greasy Chevy vans, filled to the breaking with sound.
"Where's your heaven now, where's your [zero] father of lies?"⁹
I will attempt to imitate by whispering names, sadly, deadly names

only. Negatively now, pulsating the ice-flow region
simply nine floors below the cafeteria grin
of sludgy proto-dancecore hairnets and much pointing,
there are thirteen billion mistakes in the gateway

waiting for that single video return to the nowspace
of extended singularity—the angels and the devils try to make it
their own—lucky break for this crystal haven that there was only
        spiderwebbing
rather than the great ballast symphony of shattered and fallen one.

vii. In that Hour of Gentleness

Delight in the simplest form: the forerunner
not hiccoughing merely bread and water lazily
past banks or near the ebb, rather a toss of the wind,
a nonchalant throw while spinning bacchanalianly
with a composure of spirit and precision in movement—
let the strata of your heart be united, even in this wild simplicity.

If one were to wish for you a moment in time to inhabit,
one single event to which everything is invested and all else
subject to, what would be that moment? The happening of things
crouches down into dawn, that first slight spark that hides
yet precludes a great immensity—would that be it?
Drunk from the rafters to the soil, exhausted by the merriment,
is this what you would be waiting for, the simplest of things
as the night heeds its beck-and-call to ideal illumination?

You always listen to that throwback nostalgia, not waiting
nor listening for new frequencies. There is a joy in driving home
while the rest of the city still sleeps and begins to wake
that cannot be contained in even the most complex moment,
a joy from without that needs your within to come to pass,
a joy you may never have had or have forgotten,
forgotten its gentle brush upon the storehouse of dawn.
Only the best is wished for you. Hope you know that.
Hope that one day you will see something ascending into the sky
and not need anything else, and not sleep for one moment longer.

B. Blame

Try not to lapse. Do not leave before
something is taken away, before the anvil light
deconstructs yesterday's little leaning into that
taste fragment underneath your tongue, that little razor.
Could she have stood? Upon the wire-mesh platform?
It was not too late, last time. Thick cords pulled from
somewhere below dragged her off, but you . . .
you needed somewhere to keep breathing,
to keep your own sauntering afloat in the miasma
I like to call the weightless unfathomable, sometimes.
You might stand on the street corner trying to hail a cab
when there is no one around to watch you stick
that same finger down your throat. The bombast
usually used to frighten is now hearing its own
(n)u(n)clear façade as a somnambulistic overture three years
before your birth. You couldn't have cornered the market
any better had you adhered to the graven images all around completely.
Slowly, the parapets are beginning to grow larger;
do not let their intimidating mirth laugh you away
from the battle, from the sea you could float in.

Late last night you crouched upon your stoop
and smoked cigarettes, exhaling them violently
at the lonely passerby or two, though they strode
a distance not even smoke could traverse.
I know. You told me and I watched you out of the corner
of my second story window as I watched softcore pornography.
Wait to judge, for a moment, while I'm telling you this;
it is all quite peripheral. The thing that mattered was that
woman being fucked on the screen, though screaming, yelling,
and flailing, was exhaling just like you. Okay, it wasn't softcore,
it was a snuff film I had bought at the swap meet—I knew
a guy, who knew a guy, who knew a password, but that isn't
even what was important—her dying breath was the same
exhalation as yours before you flicked your cigarette into the street—
your landlord gets upset when you leave them on the steps—
you may have stopped believing in coincidences, I certainly
have. And then. And then I was watching you, watching me,
watching the screen watching you, while you read this over
my shoulder, and didn't believe a thing, because you knew
there was no possible way for me to get my hands on something so vile

as a reader who would think for a moment what it would
be like to a) watch a snuff film, or b) be in one. But we have.
We all have. It was a day not too many years ago, and we'll
all see it again, again, again. But that isn't what was important.
And that I cannot remember. But that isn't what was important either.

What *is* important: the bane of the carousel
revolving and revolving, what *is* important, the cataracts
now sealing up your ears, nose, asshole; what *is* important:
the catalepsy that seized your body overnight but was
gone, instantly, when the first light hit the east; what *is*
important: the medical condition that they haven't
been able to name or diagnose, much less find
victim (or cure) for; what *is important*: the last time
you stopped, the last time I told you not to leave, though
you did, the last time the figures underneath your
fingernails finally added up and then were quickly forgotten;
what is important: the fastidious way you never ever
quite put your cigarette out all the way and it seeps
its unused smoke into the room, the party; *What Is Important*:
the miles of used up soda cans we can attribute to you
in the landfill, the dandruff you spilled on my coat in the middle
of the best scene in the movie before you leaned over to teasingly
drop the razor into my neck, the fixation with mothballs, the
quiet dreaming and the loud, the forlorn and the saved, the
mystery drink used to knock her up, the dressing table the next
morning after your first real forced penetration, the nighttime
lauding of heaven and earth, the occultism lining your and my
shelves of desire, the transgression I feel when you forget
to rip out my nipple-ring just right, the libertinage feeding
off your backside, the exultant misery of exploded buildings,
the damaged singer from some all-night band playing their sidereal hymns
    to the zombies,
the zombies, the walking dead you have summoned for your own
    purposes,
the recreations around the time the precepts of physics stopped applying
to anything, the laudanum you slipped in *everyone's* drinks
that one night, the time you let me believe that I had ultimate access
to an orgy I had no right to be at, the time I tortured you mercilessly,
neither hearing the cries of your parents and children as they looked on
nor my own wracking sobs as I let the diamond lined piano cords strangle
your limbs while I click-clacked away, the time I let you dip a pen into my
    eye

to write the only love poem anyone has ever given me, the anarchist we
    met
and threw to the ground, spat on, and said, "there's your motherfucking
    anarchy,
swine," the thing we possessed, the truth in using a stiletto for artistic
    purposes,
the last great performance-piece cum suicide, the goddamn end of the
    world . . .
what is important are none of these things because they did happen
    somewhere.
What is important is the feeling you are having right about

now.

Do not lapse. Do not fear your own implication.
Do not leave yet. Tarry on, for things

V. Evening and Morning, Drunkenness and Dreaming

spoiled[40]　　　　　　　may be
　　　　　　　& what to ask for?
　　　Triumph
Veer quick lodestone friends
paltry are the turnips turned in the sod for gusto and schmaltz
quick　　　　　& wait,
　　　I'm a bad parentage stultifying DJ,
this is why the striding quietude gets
oh, turned　　　　　Jasmine & Ruled^r
what about Maybelline on the concourse, on the jet-pack
　　　　dendrocrenologist,
on the get off the boat before the haphazard wave comes, the pick-up-
time, the forgotten course of dr[▼]op the bombast!
　　　& the explosions.
Jacoby & the passion of re-gifting.
Like a heartbeat, water infus[s]éd
going nowhere & like the "water-to-wine-party" we always meant to
　　　　throw,
like the lost feeling of failure,[41]
it was only a throne-ness that upbraided our all too constant *misgivings*.
And what of it Miss Crematorium? Nothing *hits*,
nothing
as if [comma] we all descended
(& what of it, you, with your hair shirts . . .)
toward Those Plans. If He only knew the plans They have for[42]
forgotten leisure.

---

[40] Temporality is the cause of any "brattiness" or "only-childishness" that may arise at this point.
[41] Whatever *that* specific word means.
[42] Sadly, us.

A. [The Baseball Description: Top of the 6th. 1 Out. (Score miserably tied.)[43]]

I had just plunked one down right over Henry "little" Seas,
tying the contest and fulfilling my option. My contract served,
I was called for the after-times, a new beginning in the big sleep
when She walked into my life off the humid, picador street,
right into the big Bermuda arms of the Hairy Monk, serving both as
Birmingham's principal place of ill-repute and the moniker I had acquired
tasting leather-cork with ash, rounding the bags as a Gamecock.

[Morning struck softly over the Alleghenies.
I let the BOB roll over me like waves of nightcrawlers.
Night descended slowly over the Superstitions.
The Show was not any bigger than I always knew it to be.]

Like any stone giant, the Show was bred upon body and water.
About as interesting as [new] critical theory in the sack,
the lactose intolerant new jubilation of distinctive characteristics
that works in the fellated lack of judgment (extreme parentage, the
        slight smile—
we who grouse upon what you have given us, we ask to control, just once)
        and
what gravitates your own so extravagant. . . .

It was not ninety feet to first that time:
it crawled, roughaged, plowéd slowédly
through the digestion of your consciousness
and your effects. If only you did not have that
thirty-eight inch hickory (which is not allowed),
cork all strung through like devil's maidens and ventriloquism.
If only you were not about as budged as
Cinderella on stalactites. On those so phallic drippings
one could hang their own red-town-painted-glories,
their renaming of hell and a distinct kind of burning.
If the true nature be not what one has always ascribed to it,
would it be more overtly correct, than not, to assume
that just past the incarnation dancing there is not some goddamned truth,

---

[43] That gross confederacy of Iowa. The game went for half-a-year and then it was erased, not only from history, but from the lay of the land. The flood that ensued swallowed up the concourse and all our wives. Children were not born but from exemplifying miracles. Hail, Elistan! The hourglass constellation is coming, and with it, ash.

some quicksilver psychrometer ready to measure our own agendas
more quickly than the best BBC/Maxwell Smart (DRAGNET)/
       HomelandSecurity
breach honed by {(wo)[sic]}man in the twilight of these last days of idols
and cenotaphs? Where then, Mighty Babe, lies baseball?

Grounded to second among the pebbles and concrete gleanings from the
       night before,
conquest was a crowding into
monster gleaming upon the bright stereophile in the crapshoot of the thin
       dialogics we propose.
Woe to cancerous incarcerates, plodded down and (oh hell) woe-begotten
       measured mistakes—
down, termiting and hogsquatting leprous indignancies to our own fetal
       perambulations.

We can allege that Brighton and Brixtol prospered, but they didn't have
       the MudHens.
Didn't have Her. Dame-bastard moving in the night.

[Intermission/Second Interlude:

One.
Two.
Three.
Four.
Five.
Six.
Seven.
Eight.

One eight six five six. Three eight four two. Four one. Four one four two two six.

Two eight six one six. Nine two eight three. Five four eight two eight two.

Fifteen minutes later. Half-an-hour. Quarter past.

Zero hour. Eleventh hour. Twenty-four hours.

One hundred dollars. One million dollars. One billion dollars.

"Knee 1." Was not supposed to be very good at the violin, that brain,

that body with that first knee and the second. E=

—Time. Does not. Exist.—

A googol.

No trixie. Four. Same root.

Lights flicker.

Return to your seat. . . .

End Interlude]

What was I to do that hot and lonely April
when I stroked your naked body one night
and the next you fell into my friend's bed never to return?
I went on a hitting streak, that's what.
The D-backs were never the same again. Three-hundred forty-three
    games.
One day off and four-hundred [emancipation dreaming:
records are . . .] ninety-two games.
Only, wait, not yet 24. Bat. avg.: .674.
832 homeruns. Do the math.
And ask yourself,
has he slept with his [insert here: family-member/friend/stranger]?

A baseball player like some cast-off prophecy,
a flouncing, dawdling,
self-eye-wounding-when-the-truth-be-told
heresy!
Daughters of law, coronate yourself,
for Creon could not stop the mutilation in the arena,
nor the praying to gods. Please. For my sake.

Too much to ask. Far, far too much.
From this one who has asked so little,
so friggin' little of anyone, except,
[redacted]! There is not enough time in this life to accomplish anything.
And yet we spend so much time—such an extraordinary amount of
    time—
upon those who have died.[5]

I was quite sick. So I retired holding every single goddamned record.
What an encyclopedia of a single name.
Such beautiful scars.
Dare I mention the word?

i. The Retired Cobb

So we have not forgotten thirty year conundrums,
so the forlorn love you sought did not come back bounding into your
        bed,
is this any reason to cry, to drink Dr. Pepper upon the evening
and wait for its laxative shift? Good for us,
you might amuse, but you know. You know the constellations are
        making everything easier.
What shall I wake to but the refuse modern,
the cunnilingually feared, the too new to be anointed,
the adroit, the cunning? You're'll so shy. Just crisp. Just breathe in the
        September air.
It is almost as if we had never talked to one another. Just curtailed up. Just
        jumping.
Falsely Victorian, woe, these peasant pushers,
these clowns of architectural ambivalence,
you and I and I clothed in only all
to loathe your ease with the world;
it is not a pretty sight, not a crawling into the belly of dawn;
it is much more like you to wish for your own dreams to drown you, to lie
        fallow
upon the brooding ground of evermore, of clandestine pushings,
than push up through that meager hedgerow, that *White Album* of failings,
that cordoning off of actual thought, you measly scum fantods.
Is it such an insult to say that I have set a record that will never be
        broken? (And you could
never even hope to paint the town red, much less rename it Hell you
        motherfuckerswine?)

B. Late in the Twenty-Seventh Inning

Fatigued, the waitress serving burgers topped with bacon and dripping fat let one small glass fall to the floor. The sound it made was as a delirium so close to the television, muted, tuned to the all-night baseball game, a game being played late in the twenty-seventh inning. The men sat at their tables, heads bowed into their food. The women sat idly picking, picking at the potatoes and lumps of meat, their hands tracing patterns into the counters. There weren't many times that wood could lavish itself like those countertops, so pristine, so many new children. Indelibly marked with an asterisk—it all pointed to the discussion had one time deep, deep in that diner; now it was so quiet that the spoons stirring the coffee couldn't even be heard—it was all clear once. All it took was one glance into the parking lot, one glance into the outside of things and all those rivets were undone: rope being dropped from the top of a ladder into deep, deep pits always marked close to the restroom with little symbols— an asterisk, of course—there, they never stopped trying even though the automobile outside had shut off its lights trying desperately not to kill any more bugs. The chef in the kitchen would whisper that orders were ready, would whisper at the food he prepared, would whisper at the knives and skillets. Once, the waitress had heard him and she brought his words to a table who were oblivious to the baseball game being played, still early in the third, and they ate his words, and their forks and knives hovered above their food, above them, above those whispered words. Now there are no words, not even swearing or cursing at the shattered glass, or the home run hit, or the cars pulling up—the men and women ordered by pointing at their menus, by pointing at their desperation marked with an asterisk: this dish is spicy. . . . In his whispering, the cook forgot to inundate his dishes with spice. The waitress, knowing this, brought bottles of Tabasco® to the tables, trying to make up for the general lack-of-anything in the air, in the food, in their hands, in their coffee, outside, inside. But this night would never end, never see the conclusion, never see a winner triumphant or a loser having lost the last great game. It would wind and unwind, vibrating, falling. The waitress would sweep up the shards of glass and dump them into the garbage. She would untie her apron and take a smoke break on the loading dock. She would stare deep into the forest behind that diner, and somewhere there would be utensils singing, singing. And somewhere there would be nothing.

VI.

A.i. Nautilus or Plotinus

If I were to describe to you exactly how I got here,
there would be very little math involved indeed; and yet,
I fear the pinecone-wobble will not break its pattern.
There is a sinkhole waiting in my backyard for a drowning.

When I was young, I would gather around another,
far-flung from the lay rhapsody of Sonoran Desert streets
(their blinding glare still burned as eternal afterimage
into the cones in my retina, smashed by the flask-handle)—

its orbit, as I waited, was the spiraling of a penny
in a dime-store receptacle to fight cancer. The loss,
after clashing with another, cried to the Fibonacci moment:
the ones and ones and twos—and a desire to pierce
the cycle I had found myself in: these nine-to-five deaths
in ten. I fear the satellites circling Earth are to become

comets of kingfisher steel as they rocket toward gravity
and our halcyon nights, fear the trace back to the beginning
leads through the center, and fear only a lightning-rod
can pierce the *māyā* that veils the mask I would wear
if I were to describe to you exactly how I got here.

ii. Volcanoes/Organics

The way things look. The manner in which creation covets its opposite.
Holding against breast and yet lacking attention, not only to detail,
but against the downward gaze of any who would wish to decorate
toward palimpsest—longitudinal distraction, latitudinal ritual
along the concentric circles growing smaller in either direction.
The equator is only *a* center flush against the bright white locks
hung above dissipating incense and the sordid affair of religion.

I wish there was an object that could hold my furious gaze
before and because a rising sun clamors into the sky
breathing its slow opiate tide of exhaustion. There are rituals,
even on the corner of my street, that I will never experience.
So many gather to wave their hands and lie their brittle bodies down
in hope of preserving even the smallest volcanic explosion, of containing
    it
right below the surface and letting the smoke drift out of their mouths.

I am always looking for how this world mirrors another, what relationship
lies in the middle of the centrifuge that throws and gathers its own,
that throws and gathers affinities like parasites on a withering redwood.
Would it not be nice to watch the stars blink out one by one:
a possibility I could dance to, get dressed up for in the most complicated
array of scarves and paint and wound round cloth, making use
of the way a body lets garments drape around it like part of itself.

What have I lost in the denial of ritual that comes so naturally now?
If it is only appearance, the appearance we all create to make everything
look as if divined, as if descended from the spheres above, as if
there was no other possibility, then I am content to lie at the bottom
looking up at the stark mad ether and the emanation from somewhere.
And if in the distance I can hear a car horn bleating its simple beat,
then the destruction has been worthwhile: the separation of these things

that can never truly be without their other but are on the round mind
of exploding ground. I have sat for days, and will again with nothing
for attention to grasp but braided hair laid at my feet. I have stood
in the middle of streets. I have supplicated my body in the smallest
of sleeping corridors—a picture of a blind man ringing a bell on the wall.
I have stared at *Baraka* and hoped to see a void but did not.

Oh what a gift the arteries of cities are—the clogged moving steel,

the bodies with direction, purpose. To shine or run from
moving tectonic plates: that could be enough for some.
But for me, landslides and avalanches of desire crease my eyes
against the glare of what I see as conveyor belts of flesh
delivering into a bay that can never be seen as struggle,
but rather an easing into the casement of habitation.

I ask that we pick through this rubble, not to tear our fingernails out,
but to find a glowing stone that has been there since the beginning,
to become tenant farmers of our own waste—an agriculture of renewal
and decay. Hoeing and picking, sowing and reaping the ground
of broken concrete and graffitied hope—not to sleep or begin again,
but for the song and accompanying dance that would spread from within
if we had not begun digging with our hands, if we had started clawing
at the very root of our slow fever of loss.

iii. If the Marianas Trench Were a Gathering of Sound

Everything would be skylights and hunkered down worries:
one penetrating the topsoil to wind adventures
in sticky radiance, an envelope of fire and salt;
the other a cascade of gummed intentions,

caramelized and static. All would be as it should be
in carbonite freeze. Even dreams would be white rooms,
starched sheets and pillows, milky and perfect.
This would be nice for a time, the time of cloudless banks

roiling above, and then there would be so much liquid.
The surface: a blank Silenus stare, but underneath would be
tributaries where movement was almost imperceptible—
a sea of palpitating limbs: kids going apeshit.

Stacked one atop the other, they would sway in time,
beating their strange hands against the roof
four feet away. The lime of the walls dripping.
A few suffocating at the bottom of the pile.

"Caution!" the walls would read: protective headgear
is required. It is a function of survival, of proliferation.
It is a function of the planet's rotation.
And then crying. Tears, disturbing the wave-break,

would find themselves in open waters, fiddling nervously
with the switches and diodes controlling the whole thing.
And the worry will disappear, even if the kids cannot see.
The movement will stop and those suffering at the bottom

will be able to rise, shake the sweat out of their hair
and look each other in the eye, silently admiring
their beautiful coral pith helmets, their perfectly made-up
coifs. And then there would be a stillness

requiring neither glue nor coercion. Rather, the only requirement
would be darkness, and there would be plenty of that.

iv. The Path of . . .

Some small piece of honey, gummed and hanging
from the kitchen counter waiting for either chemicals
or a chemist to come along and assure it of a long
descent toward the infinitesimal floor, a rest stop
on its consuming path that is no birthright of generations
(even if it be of the great engendering drop),
was lost from the fold of proliferating Turing machines,
lost for its untimely pastness stamped on a hardened viscosity
with some Lot's signet ring also given to remunerative imploring
of the regalness of a past's canceled debts.
What is asked for, swaying imperceptibly in the slight breeze of breath,
was simply the defenestration of another word for psychoanalysts
until someone came along and plucked it off
with tweezers that smelt faintly of a vengeful urine,
and flushed it down the toilet with the rest
of the spume, bile, and mucous,
until it found the rhythmic river it desired
in the flow of swirling and rising melody
deep in the most life-abundant, vegetal overflowing
of chasms, where no light reached
save its own amber beckoning and sweetness.

v. An Unlikely and Heretofore Unseen Calm

A harbor, conceding particular dockings,
I have frozen over, an inlet
not allowing vessels to be worried
even on the departed fluctuation of my rocking.
Where did the flame go
that kept this port open for weary travelers?
My coasts have not been ravished
nor wharves corrupted; this winter
has not been overly cruel.
No wind came a-snuffing,
and yet, everything is crystalline calm.
To ask for a thaw, a melting
to get these ships off to sea,
or even more ice . . . but not this,
not this perfectly defined horizon (that is me),
this perspective momentarily blinded
by the brightness of reflected light only . . .
to see—to see an infantile non-motion—nothing
moving against the now cracked
and splintered bulwarks. All the cargo
has been unloaded, the crews put-up,
the night's drunken brawls growing larger
for landsickness. All of everything has been done
that could be done in the face of such a freezing,
for the town has prepared for this, prayed for this.
Why then, why in such blatant answer,
is the town asking more of me, why does it desire,
why does it hope, change, facile and inconstant,
in the blinking northern light of consciousness
for. . . ?

VII. Oceanic: Theses on the Abuses of Indexicality (A Narrative of the Hyperarchive)

A. Oceanic

When first the penultimate moment between clawed sky-hammer
and pitch clay cried, rid of its previous natality, the forgotten gills
were the tale of Encyclopedia folded into a bottle
to set sail against the sun from mirror inhabited isle.

In need of a herald, the threshold of electrocuted engendering
gathered its claxon trumpets and hollow-eyed standard-bearers,
their grieving first breaths lamenting the ubiquity of the sea,
and smashed a bottle of nectar on the analog bow of departing
        information.

Where negation might lie, the reflexive move capsized,
voided, before any binary coupling could occur, by the horizonless
field of multiple beginnings. Each curled dimension was allowed
to explore the plotted points of its own memory, unfurled along

axes of incalculable data, until the unraveling coalesced
into indivisible matter with no entry points. All of this occurred
in the wake of an already disappeared and swimming hyperarchive,
an ultrachronicle of this used-up [. . .]-verse. The grains of sand

froze over and the beach dissolved into concrete and the cables
of parallax fantasy were not permitted any books to scan,
any documents to file or shred, but kept ticking away
their lonely banshee note in realized singularity. They were left

only the task of describing this singleton before the last evental
careen could lay unmeasure to rest by a closing of incompleteness
and measureless standing reserve. Nothing left to do but await
the worlding of some vague appointment in the briny darkness.

B. Indexicality

> *Veracity thus has two sources: being, which multiplies the infinite knowledge of the pure multiple; and the event, in which a truth originates, itself multiplying incalculable veracities. Situated in being, subjective emergence forces the event to decide the true of the situation.*
> —Alain Badiou, *Being and Event*

PURE MULTIPLE:

The locks on starry-night vault;
above, a syrup flooded bathroom.

        A shapeless eye underneath the combination—
        from it grow masses of tiny hairs.

            Someone banking on the morning
            put down roots on the rim of Flatland
            and refused to look over the side.

Why him? Why was he chosen for this? For making a widget in Saskatoon
    to become the central component of a deathmachine buried three miles beneath
    the desert?
There *were others* in the carpet.

        A puppet, dangling his legs over a hand,
        missed the opening ceremony celebrating the
        anniversary of his own ascension.

(These fragments are only uninterpretable representations in the reflexive
    nature of. . . .)

          The sad day when even puppets require
          a *nom de plum* with which to accord
          to the requisites of autonomasia . . .

              . . . holds down the body without
              by means of razor lined straps
              to get at the glass frozen inside.

Look at the massive ball the dung beetle rolls.
It is a mixture of buildings, tourniquets, and dreamy demonstrations.

          This satellite, urging rising to its monstrous gravity,
          follows the railroad tracks in the door

        to the brig of perception

                (inside the stockade of your eyelashes
                that contain liquid nitrogen
                with which to bind the movement

        of the much smaller, cube-shaped
        gaol in the corner of the even smaller
        restitution camp, but only as a detention center
        for those refusing the inscribed exit strategy)

    upon which it looses all the accumulated
    hand tools stolen from the artisan's grasp.

Can the ambient noises be heard?
What is arriving out of the fallow-land?

        If wont to essay the burning limb strapped to the bed
        arises desire in a hunched love-sprocket

                sing "best-me-down along the way";
                the nails have been removed
                from the hands of the destined
                silently trilling children around

                the carousel of the word for the day
                that will follow the day after
                one finally realizes that they have
                fallen out of the graces

                of their own love for (an)other.

VERACITY: $\{n \rightarrow ?_n$. Consequently, there also exists the union-set of this set; that is $?_{(?0)} = \chi[?_0, ?_1, \ldots ?_n, ?_{n+1}, \ldots]\}$ • Knowledge from above $\emptyset$

The Event that has been placed in a bottle and sealed off from the fidelity
    of the world.

C. IOPT

The slow going toward perception that is caused by the gap in binary, digitized time has not only been caused by the term *Index of Petty Tragedies* (IOPT), but it has left its fragmented nature to be inscribed upon the very condition of cognition from which that perception was originally thought to be possible. The problem then is not housed in the IOPT itself, but rather somewhere in the multiplicity of what is, if anything can be said to be, outside of it. This very outside, if possible, is the must-ness of possibility, or rather, that only-ness of what is left. For the very condition of positing an outside already presupposes that there is something to be outside of, and consequently affirms the interior of the not possible inside-ness. Or to put it another way, for there to be an outside and an inside there must be a position from which to name a condition inside (everything not being in that condition being outside). The problem with finding this position is, of course, the very problem with infinity. Infinity is, by its very nature, multiplicitous; there are infinities greater than others, which also mean that there are an infinite amount of possible infinities. Then the problem with these infinities does not revolve around an attempt to measure them, but rather to define a position from which one can say that this infinity is larger than another: the zero point on the line of infinities. So again, to speak of an inside and an outside requires a position from which the binary can come into focus.

Just like the problem with binary language (1s and 0s), however, there always remains an unknowable (parallax) gap between these two terms, or rather, what ≠ 1 or 0. So if we say outside = 1 and inside = 0, then there is a necessary term that has been left out, namely, what is neither inside nor outside, a third term that would designate the very place from which we could name the two. Now this third term will of course designate a multiple, but a multiple that neither belongs to inside or outside, and thus the count of this singleton gets its name: IOPT. The strength of using this term as it has just been defined is that it frees IOPT from being inside *or* outside—i.e., it is not outside the outside, nor inside the inside, nor even in any measurable relationship to the two terms, nor even anywhere quantifiably *else*—so we can use it freely without having to worry about the fact that it is semi-indefinable. Its strength as a term is caused by its indefinable-ness. This might strike one as incoherent or contradictory, but if we are to begin to explore the nature of the relationship this term has to digitized time rather than the good ole' analog time of the twentieth century, there must be a horizon opened up that does not *totalize*, the intuitable fact that, say, *The Matrix* showed so clearly: it is impossible for the superstructure of the digitized world to maintain itself, or more possibly, that the very organicity of the world denies the complete and utter totality of digitized (almost-absolutely-measurable) time—there *must* (at least hopefully) be a condition of time that stands in relation to the very multiple of multiples that, at the very best, can be counted but never measured.[t] It is this term we define as the IOPT.

D. Don't Sweat the Small Stuff: Burn the Fucking Library

This thing, this catalog, this archive feeding weakly
upon its own principles of maintenance and proliferation,
I am but the lonely clerk of, a bygone by epigone no longer allowed
to walk amongst the stacks nor fraternize with the other departed;
and this has been my blessed task:

>   account for the catalog
>   that has traversed its first principles,
>   has become the excessive remainder of itself;
>   and the sliver of itself it contains within itself
>   can only become Thing by this obscene excess.

I seem to catch blundering and imagistic hints
of a not ill-defined horizon, a towering building, finite
within an architecture devoted to exploding previous limits
(but whose liminal transgress was *not to be written*),
whose first three floors were dedicated to organization

and the rest devoted to maintaining and continuing its decimal logic;
and I can remember an inferno of departing informatics.

E. A Not Too Thinly Veiled Critique Against the Ametascientific "Newness"

What forlorn beast should shelter me
if, having given in to the redemptive pleasures of things,
the night could weave all the interstices
of the word for the sound of falling coins
and water droplets together into a general theory
of simultaneity and synchronicity, except an-
other kind of libertinage undiscussed and forbidden
underneath even the most transgressive of modes,
without which, whose dream has misted over the
lenses of our seeing with heat, even the moons
remain absent?

The last call I made toward the horizon
of tired syntactical semblance returned
these more and more unanswerable questions,
these fits of dandelion fur in the grill of a car,
but failed the space in front of one's
mouth, which there also desperately needs to be
a word for. Cleft palette behind it, not for
lack of breath or bodily harm, but the simple
dying of the tongue in its own glorious juice-
bath, it accedes to undertake at every moment
of an outpouring: a going up and down. Still,
I do not labor on, emptied and destitute, but
am at the height or depth of an inching toward
what may be called an evolutionary need,
a drying of parchment outside this mollusk-
wet and cantankerous hurdy-gurdy of millennial
vapors. The sad old angel of history has not
veered from her path or vision, but has now
agreed to only relate the storytellers' telling
stories about telling stories, disenfranchising—
under the detritus of a yet different mode
than the transgressive—those who refuse
to even relate the here and now anymore at all.

The amateur field of open beginnings
is not anymore the subject of documentary realism,
but nonetheless has succumbed to a certain abuse
of Alexandria. I lift with my shoulders all the

weight of it I can handle, and yet want more
while fearing the rolling-up, the piling on,
the energetic and exponential accumulation.
The alabaster and the barges are now fraught
with storms in the pilaster of their passing voyage.
Their foghorns, though now unnecessary, have,
of course, ceased to function, replaced by tiny
circuits and bread—the growth of the rotting
and enveloping deep, the brief and carbon-monoxide
absorbing vastness that reaches its hands
all around this sentimental weariness, refuses
to be caught into its own invectives. The
birth of the new weightless ballast has never
been closer at hand nor further from mind;
the old idols are returning, thankfully,
but are becoming, as they once were incapable
of being, true lords of creation, gods for whom
the entirety of the human is verifiable and at hand,
for those who would read this crazed palimpsest
wholly, for they are the only ones. Be careful
where you set down your book of matches young one.

F. Saguaro

Upon my languishing arc,
my torso ubiquitous and liquored,
an expression of pure multiple
is finding another kind of index.

I'd salute my planter if he
were not this box I while away in, trading
draught for a prick and ribs for a draught.
How might I fare if yon clay held a bit more manna,
or if your teeth, fair tusked one, could stomach my
melodious offering of arms bearing fruit.

(Turn me over in my bunk-sect and
release various decoding programs
into the drizzled light.
Farther on, wake.)

There is secobarbital in the drought
and plows escaping handmen in the flood—   The grasp.
wherefore art thou cutlassed spine-maiden   And irresolution.
and infecund wash? I'm setting upon this
desert fit for kings, but brine is collapsing barnacles
against my hull and fibrous skin. I prey (upon) harpoon gales(,)
in their NaCl wisdom, could find me all the readiness,
but a last guffaw at the edge does not hear nor a precipitate remain.

G. Access: Denied

Feverish culmination and fingernails ignored,
the goddamn rhetoric eased its French exit
from the room of refusing to open files,
from there where damage=delicious libraries.
"Expunge," it said to itself while the doorjamb waited,
"expunge the fascination of malevolence
through a 'never having listened to before'
dancing/waiting derivation cued by simple,
all too simple, desire—and razors. A lot of (a shitload of) razors.
And screaming." The party it left
had by that time used up all the nicotine swill
given by the untoward visions of eternal
"we'll get back to that next time"
simpering on the lawndeck of a very necessarily open bar.
The result: catastrophic amalgamation:
closing the debtbooks before they've been paid:
mistletoe dreaming on the backside
of this history as streetwalker, history
as the chemistry of your last forgotten love affair.
Mister, or so he'll be called from now on,
was not noticed upon departure. Rather, Mr.
was lostness in the lake of his own infinity,
the *gerimandisos* of forgetting in racketeered penumbra,
the "one more step and you die"
message of what From Monuments to Masses have been spreading
like disease, like painted over Bombergs (thankfully)
in this half-leavened violence of waiting—
one would wish to not be subjected to
in the [why is this record so quiet, it is supposed to be
metal] clamor of opposition, to what stands so "culturally"
divided, basically, well, from freedom in all its incarnate glory
on the backs of goddamn giants succeeding where
screeching fails—consequently picking its easy sides
counter to the dreaming on the moribund fabric
of the consequation of landscape mixing its nettles in:
all easy fantod in the counter-reversal of mores—
one would ask for at least an exit,
a possibility that lying had forgotten itself
in that strange moment of commitment and
lessening of constellations, that someone (at least)
had discovered a slim possibility, a chance,

to not be subjected to the insane rule of tomorrow;
and descending like so many crystals
into the lakebed of eternally returning vomitation,
everything got very purple, bruised in the night-evening
fact that no one (singularities defunct), no one at all
noticed the right-left of leaving from the
honey-warehouse-flytrap-disco-insomnia
of all of us gathered together asking for one more day and
having decided upon one last question:
where did that dame-bastard wander off to?
(I was supposed to give him/her/it a ride home.)
Decided it was all for the better
to do one last bit of forgetting.

H. Ode to the Quadratics of Soprano-Voiced Mathematicians

Miscalculations to the lakefront,
hands held and heads nervously circling,
these are shores first seeking the soles of your ancestors
and they are not asking for a drowning.
Miscalculations wading shin-deep
into the mire—benefit of error,
cradle of instructors—wash the soiled sheets
of your parting upon the whetstone-
sheath of an eternal return, and forgetnot
to circle the short-circuit path while
keeping your distance.

There are abominations in the forest, so
beware the gloaming sent to bind your hubristic hands
and lay-faculties structured around your French inhale.
You would be vampiric entropy for the moss-bite
laden upon carnage sought if not for
slight gaps in assurances displayed and funereal.

This is all to say:
for one receiving instructions,
be not stranded in your own incoherent formulations
while the staged procession carries on;
be not self-conscious of the token for the ride home;
it rests in your back pocket quite nicely aware
of its own fragility and frail expression.
Do not refuse to ask questions from unsublimated heights
of rusted out old idols and visions of eternal youth
dusted of the answer of death refusing the questioning answer of life,
for the opposite acknowledgment of resisting answers
mixes the desideratum paleshadow-ploughshares
on its own good way, in its own good time;
and I ask you forego misapprehending your value

and transvaluative potter's wheel's coherence
to the spinning jenny of your dot matrix-scrawled thoughts.
The hair on the back of your palms is burning.
The clock face watched nuzzles its fiction in the smell.
Palliatives are not consuming your math
and you are not watching stumbling multiplicities,
evental and leaving, rock their cocoon in the free-wheeling reign

of bordered null-sets in the realm inscribed but
forgotten in powers of simulated forgiveness.

Miscalculations, heed your beck-and-call
to the fires of individuation. Miscalculation
(heed that ceaselessly ringing church bell),
your pitiful survival through adaptation
[wait] almost negates arboreal-city-truth.
For that, no trust. No clamoring. No
sleeping with your own felicitous children:
nausea, indictment, caprice, neurosis, and ire—
not to mention their spouses:
fornication, forbearance, patience, misery, and complication.
Have you not heard, fair-haired wrongness, that
the shape of despair rests squarely on your massive shoulders?
Have you not heard that your own careless infinity masks
the night-moment of indeterminacy?
I will not live for your death fair-headed,
golden, and lion-maned angel of distress,
quiet painting, appearance foreboding, calamitous ritual,
you, you, Miscalculation. The Dionysian orgy of. . . .

Dawn. Daybreak over the Catalinas [citric acid of mountains]:
repetition—difference playing in the ultimate:
the waiting water, but full of sulfides and miscalibrated barometrics—

creates the gradual saturation of musing upon your origins, faithful
        sweetheart
[Miscalculation is bygones by epigones. There is no salvation in searching
        for the bleeding, puking heart,
unless (masked and anonymous) the flowing cape of sludge, death-growls,
and the acceptable limit of empathy, permits *exactly this wading that you are
        capable of.*
The lake is not experience. Honey, it's not even historical perspectivism,
let alone *material widening* "so that the *passage* is a city, a world in
        miniature"[u]],

your leave-taking was expected. You were hung on the cross of your own
Event, and it was a smashing,
an acoustical refrain from determinism,
a call in the darkness to an androgynous[v] "not a friend at all"
while the lakebottom called its Arthurian ridiculousness.

The poem is a call to[44] the same sort, damned
in the first movement of an orange symphony
of "dead flag blues." The poem is a cavalcade of last days
approaching testament.
The poem lies out of its spitted teeth, drunk for the first time in hours,
Horusing up to the Combat Wounded Veteran, saying goodbye to
an overture without climax,
all prelude and television
in a home of all too familiar waiting;
the poem nixes its own infanticides readily, all too readily,
while Mr. Pythagoras was outlasting the dreaming.

When you met the waters of time, what could you ask
but for at least one moment of consideration, one
ambiguous crushing, one t-shirt reading: fuck guilt?
But a rising was inevitable, a raising upon the dais of—well,
funk[w] might not mitigate its cocaine simpering, but it sure does
coalesce—a splinter, which is the best microscope.

---

[44] No, not Eurydice's side.

I.i.a. Future Journal

—After the Morningside Firestar Chat: 29 November 2056
    0258

Down on the nicotine farm. Pale for lunch today.
Saw golden cuirasses floating above New Southern
Pompeii. Jenngrün transnetted, filling tomorrow
with fertile fields, while listening to third-wave operatics
on ISSR^x-high-bandwidth. Can't sleep tonight,
too many wavelengths on the low-pressure system coming in
from the east. Synchronic symptotes confusing the
consistent. I heard the Screaming again today.

Forecast: A mild reconnoitering with the past.
Chance of tears: twenty-three over fifty-four.
Or at least that's what the air said.

My son wanted to learn the xylophone today.
He didn't know what wood was nor stainless steel.
He's thirty. Born on the Eve of Exponentia, his birth
heralded another. It is a strange time when the birth of prophets
is prophesied. S-D972^y was on particularly good terms today
with the economy, its GIQ^z risen on the index fourteen Heraclituses.

Per-Annum-Tax-Entry added into the archive today, a facsimile:

b. Recently Discovered! Pre-Consolidation Auto-Analog-Bio Found!

Though the reestablishment of personality 11.4.anarchoam.ne.bg.gmsfa won't occur until sometime tomorrow, this reporter has had an exclusive with the downloading record. Of special note in this collection was a certain penchant for dearth-veiled rmp'd discs.[aa] Among these: the screaming records of the late-twentieth, which a broad survey of will be the subject of this report,[bb] WEI[cc]:

There used to be a moment in time when knowledge was so restricted to people that they actually had to sit around listening to records together, and this constituted (one of) their primary activity(-ies). It might even seem as if everything else these people did was to enable just this kind of knowledge-/aesthetic-based-socialization, or what we call today EA (enjoyable assimilation). Well, interestingly enough, some of the records found in subject 11.4.anarchoam.ne.bg.gmsfa are beyond this reviewer's

ken. I was surprised myself when struck[dd] by the near unassailable limitation to assimilation that these discs presented to the hyperarchive. After a few perusals, however, the matter is, of course, quickly straightened out. There is a meat interaction program that is absolutely necessary, strangely so neglected these days. It can be found [
]. [End transmission.]

i½.

Back to the fields tomorrow. Thus ends today's unarchive.

ii.

—*End Serenading and* Anders Leben *Reflection-Time: 14 March 2057*
    1136

Much has changed, of course, since the singularity came into being much faster than anyone anticipated. I'm uploading tomorrow. I do not regret leaving these refreshing fields. It was inevitable in one form or another; and I don't know whether or not to be thankful that I am livdying when I am. At least in burning this there will be something lost.

J. To Imagine the Radically Other

Suspended in a raster of concomitant forms, the rarefied atmosphere
tongues your similarity[45] to those which you are of a part, and only
the parallactic space between your cells gives any indication of
        difference.[46]
If it could be called consciousness[47] on some other planet,

your lyric being communicates exclusively in the electromagnetic[48] realm;
and there is no barium left over when your nucleus is bombarded, rather:
shimmering hints of an evolved, techno-organic[49] plate of [rice grains]
and a miasmic harmony of merely implied frequency.[50] The multiplicitous

bodies and organs cannot be your horizonless[51] field of beginning—
        there,
sets have their evental[52] careen before striding within (the[Ø]void)—; your
infelicity is a becoming and reward for the twin peaks of failed ubiquity.[53]
You are only standing reserve. You are only ontopostother. You are only

marginalia. You are stranded at the end string, vibrating its tenth
        dimensionality
into eleven parsecs of enclosed space: liminal vacuum totality.

---

[45] saimlirtiy
[46] dfreifecne
[47] ccsinosunoses
[48] circles
[49] Möbius strip
[50] light
[51] Gödel's
[52] incompleteness
[53] fails

There is no representation,
no approach to this ethereal
fragment of the imagined alien.
The midget from Lynch's
maroon curtained dream
can be understood,
only one plateau,
one emanation from above
on this fallen ocean of absolute zero.

"Minor
'mode' . . .
tonal
music . . .
decentered
runaway
fugitive . . .
nonsonorous . . .
rhizome"

K. The Deca(y)des

The reels of forgotten film-stock once lining the Salt Road
contained no images of lost children or basements in angels.
Stitched together with camphor and lye
and exposed to triboluminescent lead, their makeup

of neodymium-glass mined below thousands of umbrellas,
americium and europium found in small gatherings
of crustaceans, and the platinum emulsion on famous corpses,
created a condition where their stability and longevity . . .

their stability and longevity . . . their stability. . . their

(the images as images. Midwest Products. Glories.
[Huh.] The repairman for the stereopticon debated dismantling
anything. Emunctory organs. The engineer for maser-
grafting disliked inevitable damage. Vitamins and Supplements

as rare-earth materials. Research and Development
consulted their becquerel measure) atomic-birth weight

looped around the corners of their own imagineered nitrate
Decasia and found immortality to be not far off
as the strips wound through their own pockmarks and riddled-
ascension. And yet it hasn't gotten any easier to watch television.

L. From DNA to CNN

Though you, the anchorwoman, say,
"This evening we offer you at least a shining raster
and exponentially reproducing reports on gladness and desire,"
all I hear are my implants muttering more prophecy:

«When in the desecrated channels of its own body[ee]
the Sixth-Extinction-Leviathan negotiates
thousands of hierarchical stairways in a universe
with no cosmological constant, crabs along vacuum
curves of sound, cannot escape from beneath my fingernail,
and is only an expression of a piece of meat:

a globule of semen that will become
the piece of the daughter of an unborn cow (whose manure
will fertilize the soil she will grow fat on) that I
will suck off with my teeth before it finds its way to the sea
(for it now resides on the tip of [redacted]'s moustache);
and tomorrow morning when it winds up in the sink
as part of my spittle [and the hair I pulled out of his head] . . .
I'll be glad it is hot enough to transcend helium; and

I'll want that regal glow of stupefaction
(that is worn near the glove of best intentions)
to form syllable-less crises in the morning
of invoking birth contracts.»

This is all to say . . . I like to flirt with you,
the officer giving me a DUI test in front of [redacted].
And *this* is all to say that . . .
I smoke cigarettes for my unborn children.

«Because biocrystalline structures
in blasted-book-landscape resemble
the Andromedan-hyperarchive of stars
become bandwidth nodes shimmering
their lusterless power, or the oversized head
of retarded baby Jesus in a Medieval advertisement
for *Grailland*. . . . Morricone will be proud.»

The night already lost its script.
You smell of sleep and tears.

M. Nothingness Introduced into the Heart of the Image

   —for John Cage's film *One¹¹ and 103*

A composition. Rays, shafts, trapezoidal quantum lea[n]pings.
Concurrent and concomitant black t-shirt holes.
Dandy lapel on the backside of gravitational bending.
Foregrounded absence buttressing, amalgamating,
backgrounded presence. Labyrinthine abyssal reflections.
Wall in front, mirror behind. Heat quotient of matter. Strings.
Their preparedness. A reference. Shape of space reacting.
Destroyed on its way to absolute floating.
Subject:
[   ]
      [   ]
            [X   ]
               [missing]
—occlusion, miasma, frankness, coalescence, and (non-)
drama—occurring, lapsing a mark in the corner of the page.
The next step is (in-)aesthetic. Relativity and mechanics
coupling. Miniscule particles stolen from the *Wake*. One('s)
emanation a rarefied pickup line, understood as reactionary after(-)math.
Grain of sand-size devolution describes the *whole*. Primordial
pinpoint grenade. Immersed in fabric. Messianic alterity
now fornicating illusions. Dangerous anti-mimesis. Quasi-complete
denumerable situations. The cave and brightness. Project.
Subject=
               [X   ]
         [non-substance   ]
      [nor void.   ]
[Knowledge suspended   ]
lacking didactic qualities. But massive editing. Slight delay.
Constellated libraries. Material. Infelicitous thought. Dualism
waging unbecoming. Fields. Inconsistent multiple.
Hacking massive amounts. Revising encoded
hypothetical forms. Everywhere a quarantine.
Sounding de-temporalized, binary departure.
Coordinating crystallization. Argument. Moment of
transclusive linearity. Forthwith a kind of blankness.
Polygonal relations, parabolic intensity, asymptotal approach.
Evolution of hydrogen. Impalpable frequency. Light.
subject.

                                                                    *

XIII.

The prescribed course,[54] the "wicker path" transcribed into carnival,[ff] is obnubilated. Anthropomorphic *destiny*, qualify your round-hide maneuvers, for everything is far more than obscured. There is no quotidian desire, no [sicman!] fossilization running its oblong course, no—wait, wait, wait for it—mustard-plugging (nor haphazard) sneaking into *all* of our sexual-deviations; no, there isn't very much at all, very much of anything. Of course, there is "nothing to see here," but this is just a case of me cavililling for the "whatever-side" justification. (Someone said something about clear prose.) The rotten dendrocrenologists failed to see *their own trees burning down*! What then? Must we all wait for the myopic misanthrope? Surely not—*what is clarity*!? Time. Correct. If that is (here) our preferred theme/subject of inquiry . . . how close can we possibly be? Quite a question.

A.

Found-ness in the parlanced line
quits its midst-brush(-stroke) with inflammatory
walkers of multitasked thrumming—a[s]certain stumbleitis
for the paths stretch through nine, ten strings of possibility,
cradling back in on themselves . . .
great fear,
great *not-quite-shrieking*
for projects neither earned nor fulfilled.
Too many resorts to waking and the unmapped
(neither cognitively, holistically, nor mathematically)
consanguineous ilk: bastardy of general concepts.
Riposte? Neither short, swift, nor bled.
To sing:
merely the expression of our anxious stupidity,
dumb-fear, and sands, and hands,
stopping.
Ich höre . . . was?[gg]

i.a.

Toying:
Toyota:
This.

---

[54] Time.

Wanking:
Sexing:
This.

All.

1.

Nought.

b.

Hopefully not.

Eternity.

[Placed in the ear-bud for multiple and unapologetic reasons.]

B. there is only one possible TitlE *ihearmycellphoneinsilenece*: **I've Needed Sleep for Too Long (or, the Ticking of Clocks in This Town Is Slow to Damn-Near-Unbearable-Crawl-Wise Pain)**

now this is what I call access [There is no avant-garde in the desert.][55]
nailbomb to the wall This provincial arrogance is starting to grate
gone, mixing the vehicle hate in This puffed-up little desert town,[56] and
　　　　　　　　　　　　　　　　　　　the puffed pelicans who reside
meadow looks: city's television glowing. in air so many insufficient fables
for how many i.wish.i repetitive dances have ceased　　told to ease their
on the now-this-is-what-I-call-inaccess:　　own cursory self-story and yet
　　　　　　　　　　　　　　　　　are never again about b. buckner

but he's far away, mercy.　　　"This is why we're always late," said the sad, collapsed
I shouldn't instruct on the　　man from yet another (perhaps more?) miserable,
rearing of qualification, nor　miserable IC. We don't/might let the contribution's
[ONEOFTHEOTHERS]　　　laughing touching face make you realize it was always so
　　　　　　　　　　　　　　far gone. No more rest, you. I wish I could say I'm
praxis. for electric/light-blue　rewriting the myths, legends, the creations, the origins
on the coming *clean* about, well:　of this t-town[-thug: there was a man so committed to
iamnietzsche. and then you　　certain illusions that he tattooed, in big ole letters,
gotta　　　　　　　　　　　　TUCSON around his neck . . .], but there isn't much
　　　　　　　　　　　　　　room for rewriting or revision when there was nothing
　　　　　　　　　　　　　　there in the first place to work with, ja know? "But this
　　　　　　　　　　　　　　is why we're always sick!"—self-same/stylized
　　　　　　　　　　　　　　gentleman, by way of some slight difference. Maybe
　　　　　　　　　　　　　　more importantly, what diabolical secretary entered in
　　　　　　　　　　　　　　"Meeting with Disappointment" into my action-item
　　　　　　　　　　　　　　list, my calendar of "Things To Do Today?"

be kidding me on the
field sobriety test,　　What fools, what sublime blinders, darkened lens
and about the ashes　of self-importance—nigh from a self-loathing [?]—
　　　　　　　　　　would be a flash of something [disgustingly] new.
[that throwback nostalgia]　　　　　　　　　　　　　　:::My albatross,
Now this is what　　not the easy punishment, the lance-corporal shears
I call access.　　of a semi-crappy haircut that these people are dealing with,
Not once wondering how,　　the yawp that is so stridently missing
just stepping in the　you won't miss it at all.　　the Nordic Scream[57]
　　　　　　　　　　　　is the only thing holding all the meager
I've been one of them, but have　hurricane straps in their swaying place.
realized it is absurd to give those thrill-seekers

of an indigestive yes, a "no need
to keep it quiet anymore"

---

[55] Though why should there be?
[56] This isn't heaven, this sucks. Because we are louder.
[57] One must remember that this is always provided faithfully by the robed, lounging, golden-haired, not Buddha, not Buddha, not Buddha, not Buddha, not Buddha (affirmationthroughnegation), but a founding member of the TSFHSB.

in the mondo-screen of sin-chronicled
youngsters. Pater-(/Mater)familias sheer
protective warmthhair to engage darkness,
to remember the old bad days, the all-or-nothing
Necromonger ancient battlefield days: The oh well Days
when this Law was a certain kind of truth.

C. Confession Fermata

> *So I will confess what I know of myself, and I will also confess what I do not know of myself; because what I know of myself I know by means of . . . light shining upon me and what I do not know remains unknown to me until* my darkness be made as the noonday. . . .
> —St. Augustine, *Confessions*

Hold   light.

Incorruptible substance
                                        only give proper names varying in signification.
Darkly, as through a glass—   powersets vs. consecrated counting
in caged (piano/organ)   preparations—
the director still held.   His horns had vanished[!?].
Abeyant obedience, but stilted,   hourly awaiting manifestation,
but cutoff: mask worn in sacristy   and penning trueblue verity.
A ubiquitous meeting informed   that the coming was expected
all through [one] groundless universe, if not embraced—
a fleeting
                                                             know thyself.
One worn note,   through this clamoring gap of *you*,
was an overture of the disappeared   godhead in the spun {Ø}.
. . . only define[d] Word=fractal   though diminished through retelling,
an absolutely false confession   was true on the forlorn backside
of a *dead sinking story*,   of this faith in numbers:
always a forgetting,   always a looking erratum moon,
"a *humiliation* of the Pharaoh,"   but in this noon
"trauma is eternal,"   there is no shadow underneath this gate
and there is *nothing* else   guarded by a horrible [brown] dwarf
seizing the chance, for   stars [are] in stasis, in unnameable void.

My confession has to approach
the utmost of epic proportions   (For the culling of memory
having dissolved any previous   taking place far from these shores
(—gesture   (again), toward anything resembling divinity:)
was lost at the opening, or the coalescence of   a life lived in earnest.
A formation tempting certain grounded limits—)   for there is no address
No name, but that of the convent: which means:
the nun rides high tonight: roll-ups of the best kind.
Too much mother,   too much Catholicism, [.↕]
too much will toward guilt and other perambulations that cease the sense
derived out of the Real mystery, once discovered, stretched over an entire
spectrum of what it meant to be in real life.

D.

                Time to   backup
                     through the only remaining
      escape vessel—
                Sun
                        a star, a potential negative infinity—
                largesse characterized by rosy(cross)—
                here is the AC,[58] what brings redemption
                to what disintegrates under its own gravity.

                        Traffic control
         over the sugar cane field
                              below:
                    let the parrots speak for themselves
         blow the constellations free of their prescribed orbits
                and con(de)struct missives laid easy bare

remix   remix   remix   remix   remix

     (foundness   and   reference[59])   a certain type of

---

[58] No, not "to our DC," rather the opposite, the negation of sonness.
[59]   1.

The will to world: droning ambient periphrasis.
Gumming the works and needle-nosed pliers . . .
Forceps! Hegemony is cross-stitched. The see
oh too—crave it, crave the midnight madness,
the run into the bar

                Red red hair used to be
        for the consonance
           we'll last enduring

                    2.

            it was a great hunt   sycophants!
            Alexander is your behemoth
                  on Etruscan steps
            for the ever after
                  mindless giving away of

                    3.

            you go stabbing yourself in the neck
            sigh of never-ending climate control

        freak out, the disestablishment chronology
        hands and a few feet of
        rope for the new nooses.
        I'm sick of spending these lonely nights
                boards were laid over
                these parking lots
                              without any care for
   terrible newness
                caustic   forensics
                        clamber up the
                and newness.

                      4.

four in a line of twenty
automatic like
sibilance wish
foundling child

                    5.

        employ his
        end neutral
        for keeps in the quiet
                          desertion
              Mnemosyne a bit of Ferguson
       Neutral tones disquieting in the morning enlightenment
        for reals

                    6.

qua mist. But veins, always so blue
leaping from   what white pebble   into
mistletoe veil and
Maya was my first and only   love   for shame
midnight again and what fantods
        new always
                      indecipherable

                    7.

        strange that to remember
            cut!

                            Nice
            not the south of
            but something   a bracelet

        for crowding leads to union
        a conquest that thought itself
        like a unit   but your generals

not separable!

8.

[Text lost. Presumed to be from Jordan/Sanderson.]

9.

baby   it isn't even   the end   yet

10.

Better yet

dismal

11.

the fortune galley of your will
                power cutlassed
            distinction Stella distinction

indeterminacy

12.

Action

            proliferating so easily, but there
            are divers
Painting

            so ease
                    contrapuntal yet holding its head
            whispering in nauseous quickening forsooth
            Desiderata
            it's beginning to take shape, isn't it?
            well
            at least he tries and it had stopped snowing

13.

a floor

14.

PanEuropeExpress   straight
the heart

15.

falling

                the limited upswing [got under it], floating in
miasmic   ControlControlControl
         Laugh a-bit,   to core the apple
    to fit peanut butter in the right hole
    to scamper   seconds
             away, and the
    lightfuserun   just on the back end of epoch
only, only performance *ēpochē*. . . .
    {[turn on the television. Downtown Julie Brown. What feelers have been put out, what tentacles of (de)affirmation? [The World Series was won, twice, a one in eighteen million chance]—what curses, what blessings, what scandals and poor choices? These sox have, of course, been washed clean—will their uniforms now reflect (the mirror stage?) this? [*One More Step and You Die*. (Roberston. Falwell. King.

---

        no craft work mistake

               16.

the machine
        in the end
    get you   forceps!

               17.

goddamn(goddamnImabrandnewman) red red hair
never the same
    so much settling
    so much not-quite-howling   many illusions shattered
            no one can be *your* ideal

               18.

Two baseball games

               19.

Scotch

               21.

        the year that made all this possible

               20.

there must be an end, right?

Letterman . . .)]. The works are *not* gummed, they are merely fiber optic: the stasis of traveling more quickly with a clearer *Weltanschaung*, with more pronounced gusto, with a fidelity to truth-content, with newer illusions—fabrication or *sceneanscene*/séance—with a realization of failed experiments/projects that are coming so close to an end to be fought against with all apparent lacking of reason.]hh

     The mistake
         for [R]eal[s][Ø]ii   is nothing less
than   Being}.
         Turning phenomenological [t](r)u[r]ns—
     BASTARDY, is not the crux—let alone the busted filament
     We have   been attempting (woe, yes only)
     to "comprehend"

There is, of course, a "will toward failure" that has been achieved so
     magnificently,
as if

conundrums were simply Dopamine©/Dramathurazizine mixing its
     (their)
     heartbreak, like fluoride, into your, yes *your*, drinking water.
     The Adornoian fragmentation is quitting too extreme.
     The "shudder" has left its (mark) appropriate place/station.
     The amount I drink/smoke/consume during these outings.
     The vinyl.
     The question [of course it has not been answered, it would not be
         a very good question if it were—of course!].

.sowheredidthegoddamntrainstop.[60]

[The station was not, well let's say, easy. It was right there. Where you (he/it/they/she) got off. Not in the orgasmic sense, though. No, never in that sense.]

---

[60] (?)

IX.

Temporality readjusts[61] to each microbial bending,[jj] each transient [indecipherable]
as the sway-left-right kicking loose of dusted attraction and the rusted rock-forth swings the rusted rock-back (engenders?) to lie as unmovable stone.[62]
These things and others are established.
These things and others are disestablished.

Why take the time to sit down at all, to let the transmogrifier be fit over the head
while the beauty sits languidly against the wall, waiting to flip the switch?[63]
Is it all just a waiting? On the backside of eternity?

What can I *not* see hunkering down in this time-of-times, this present?
There is war. There is not war.
There is no cat. There is no bag. There is a cat. There is a bag.
I don't see any method . . . at all.
The method is as clear as, well, morning.
[The hurricanes are getting more powerful every year.]
What.

Is it too banal to say, "We all die"?

(It was his chair.
He sat in it, rocking.
That does not change a thing.)

A thing is changed by a force, which end-times are not.[kk]
What has been gifted, must be returned. What has been made, though, cannot be unmade,[64] and that has been our gift:
to make, to change, to create, to form, to draw out of the *æther* and void a set (though never *the* set-of-sets, that would require an immortal hand;

---

[61] When Daylight Savings Time hits (other *times* as well . . .). When it hits again, and again, and again. Pinnacles and limits. Even the blessed and blessing shoppers must account for what has been imposed upon them twice-a-year with something other than the guardians in their pockets—their Roman legions—with a physical altering of the limit of the date. This is not a fucking metaphor. Goddammit this is real. Though, to be perfectly honest, Arizona has eschewed temporal shifting. . . .

[62] This would be the drone genre.

[63] Look to the sky. Ashes are falling.

[64] And vice-versa.

there have been none),⁶⁵ and we must return it, for it has only been on loan.ᴵᴵ

Everything follows the will of the great magnet.⁶⁶

As we near ends, more must be explained, more must be made clear, more must be laid bare, more must be explicated.⁶⁷ All is a lessening, however.

All.⁶⁸

---

⁶⁵ Or if there has been One, the family name is "Destroyer."
⁶⁶ See footnote [ ].
⁶⁷ More must be footnoted.
⁶⁸ Overflowing abundances (outflowing jubilations, effluvia of tragedies, of lives, pains, wearinesses, castrations,* meditations, narratives, preludes, postludes, elegies, birthdays, [slant-]rhymes, aesthetics, theories, sentences, stanzas, teachings, Socratics, shrugs, wheels,† infinities,‡ letters, collections, films, traces, questions, nouns, histories, truths, answers, sports, plays, children, pedagogies, friends, poems, nations, people, Platonists, races, weepings, genders, absolutes, (mis)readings, anxieties, influences, politics, libraries, (neo-)Hegelians, seers, prophets, religions, books, musics, families, colors, dreams, priests, "gods," births, Kantians, philosophies, studies, victories, losses, wars, *pax*, authors, visions, women, figures, novels, works, Heideggerians, pimps, pieces, photographs, magazines, etcetera(s), records, tears, dates, times, months, years, days, seconds, Husserlians, minutes, centuries, equations, beauties, uglies, cigarettes, drinks, drugs, healths, shits, doctors, lawyers, goods, professionals, white-collars, paintings, sculptures, epics, pornographies, Derrideans, aphorisms, maxims, stars, heavens, hells, planets, galaxies, universe(s), voids, abysses, One(s), Real(s), gods, footnotes, evils, manifestoes, anthropologies, sociologies, essays, Foucauldians, millennia, arguments, denials, days, nights, Christians, numbers, kings, presidents, gigolos, leaders, senators, congressmen, parliaments, governments, monies, credits, banks, energies, "angels," avatars, deconstructionists, pasts, fucks, futures, phalluses, Buddhists, speeches, debates, Americans,§ words, humans, dawns, subjects, twilights, Nietzscheans, light-years, morals, slaver(ie)s, Adornoians, dragons, bitches, universities, jobs, statistics, votes, polls, (post-)structuralists, worlds, hates, melodies, harmonies, schools, homes, hospitalities, (neo-)Nazis, nothings, consciousnesses, everything(s), multiples, Žižekians, animals, lists, games, marriages, videos, televisions, cocks, shows, legs, Benjaminians, channels, dinosaurs, wastes, receptacles, foods, blue-collars, bodies, Hindus, minds, dictators, medicines, liquids, holidays, oceans, Deleuzians, cherubim, revolutions, mythologies, Stalinists, myths, hall-of-famers, divorces, canonizers, things, marionettes, encyclopedias, legends, pets, dictionaries, Taoists, thesauri, bibles, sacraments, prostrations, objects, end-times, devices, Bergsonians, tools, mathematicians, de Mania(cs)(ns), writers, love(r)s, mouths, celebrities, individuals, stores, customers, employees, Lacanians, originalities, banalities, notebooks, rappers, diaries, journals, insects, Muslims, birds, comedies, arms, Indians, Freudians, gamblers, cowboys, comedians, gangsters, heroes, villains, damsels, Trotskyites, hosts, discussions, conversations, allowances, Jungians, tongues, wages, divisions, penetrations, breasts, (mis)understandings, lynchings, judgments, beasts, Ma[r]xi(sts)(ans)[pads], acknowledgments, Scientologists, clitorectomies,

What is the unveiling so stridently wished for?[69, 70]

---

humors, jokes, dances, condiments, cliques, clichés, generalizations, Lenninites, specifics, waters, harvests, seasons, fantasies, cycles, shambles, rambles, assholes, mothers, activists, protesters, commonplaces, communists, socialists, fascists, MCs, democrats, republicans, conservatives, liberals, companies, corporations, streets, cities, counties, countries, candies, clitorises, elbows, limbs, knuckles, fists, furies, banshees, Jews, muses, emperors, deities, blindnesses, insights, façades, symbols, realizations, illuminations, cremasters, enlightenments, Nirvana(s), anthropomorphisms, Zarathustrians, Zoroastrians, Cabbalists, devils, fragmentations, *avant gardes*, *après gardes*, chronicles, blood-lettings, brumaires, eithers, ors, *hors d'oeuvres*, demons, subjects, objects, dishes, get-togethers, fundraisers, souls, animists, deists, dialectics, critiques, (post)colonialisms, feminists, furies, Cartesians, Gödelians, (post)modernis(ts)ms, contemporaries, apprentices, *katamari*, guns, wakings, dreams, cuts, limbs, names, wests, easts, warriors, sins, matrices, clubs, fights, cinemas, puppets, anthologies, compilations, lists, cellists, treasuries, (re)inventions, appointments, boards, responsibilities, fates, historicisms, seminars, confederacies, leagues, republics, democracies, oligarchies, strangers, methods, pendulums, chairs, beds, rings, pissings, portraits, origins, theorems, fruits, meats, vegetables, grains, roots, fertilizers, theologies, gates, walls, antidisestablishmentarianisms, ch-ch-ch-changes, rock stars, moves, prayers, creatures, Things, fluids, apocalypses, Armageddons, eschatologies, genocides, holocausts),** fathers, and deaths,

sap.

* EventhethrowingofCronos'genitalsintothewaterkind. . . .
† Of time. [Of course.]
‡ Negative and positive.
§ There are "reasons" for only including one nationality. No apologies.
** This is surely not to apologize for leaving something(s) out (even the OED is incomplete . . .), but, "the will toward encyclopedianism ultimately results in the most fragmentary schizophrenia. The human mind, even an imagined 'collective' human consciousness, is incapable of containing the world. One can imagine that if in fact *everything* were to be found in one place (i.e., the Internet)—the capacity for logic, reason, knowledge, abstraction—all would be snuffed out 'like a candle in the wind.' However, right on the brink of totality, there is still the possibility of a gap, a lack, a gesture with which to hide the Nothing. *This* limit, this edge, this is desirable, or the approach of it is at least. For there is no greater goal for the human project than complete obliteration through total dominance" (Bardo Lièr Parté, "Forgetfulness: Misanthropic Glee in the New Apocalyptic Aura," in *The Crisis of Encyclopedianism in the Early Twenty-First Century: A Study of Totality and Eschatology* [Tucson, AZ: University of Southwestern Arizona A & P Press, 2007], 564.)

[69] And would it even be desirable? Would we enjoy what we see, or would we roll down the window and see nothing but an expansive gray almost-mist extending infinitely? *I* desire a mixture of this and the retention of our petty illusions. Lahaye and Jenkins have different ideas. Jerks.

[70] Or a better question: can we really footnote the apocalypse? Better to see Appendix II.

A.	[Bottom of the ninth, two out, full count, bases loaded, down by 3. Game seven of the World Series. Last ever to be played.]

It's so quiet here.
Sure have made quite a mess out of things.
Shot the sheriff and the undertaker too.
At least we have our myths and legends.

How many times that winter did I drive up Euclid Avenue
scarfing the dry ice-map of Tucson's desert streets,
drowning in red red hair, or carping the INTERPOL database, looking
 for that ruby smile-flash,
singing about lonely nights and exercises in apathy, encountering Vision?

We will go to Australia via Alaska. Take the ferry.
We'll raise sheep on the Montana plateau, the Rocky Mountain Shore.
We'll invent new . . . new demarcations of the old and foreign.
We'll have to. The Gulf of Mexico will have swallowed the Americas.

Jordan will be our Achilles. His silhouette our coat of arms.
Will someone have provided a Rosetta Stone,
a monument not subject to the price of gasoline?
Will it have been written on acid-free paper?

Will we lament the loss? Or share in the light glowing off the ice-floes?
Will we have all left the stadium content, knowing that our team did all it
 could?

[*Last Line (Drive)*: Grand Slam, and One.]

Afterword/Postlude: New Problems in the Synchronic, New Questions for the Haptic, the Spatial, the Festering Body

How much space/matter we have wasted.
Whether it be that stumbling indeterminacy of inches,
      that whittling away while fall feet-yards,
          a *( )* of miles, of light-years on the living room rocking chair or
          sweeping down the spiral-hole of the falling looking glass ride,
          the rest condemned to the wonder(waste)land of
                anthropomorphisms and mutation. . . .
      Whatever it be, there is no single space that is truly accounted for,
no *here* to spring faultless into cold calm and fecund defecation,
          an emptying
          of bowels and everything they contain: the only thing that is truly
              ours.[71]
How much space/matter we have wasted.

---

[71] Even if only for a *moment*.

Appendix I: Train Song II[72]

> Disclaimer: I have limited myself to the following things that appear. Any branching that might occur can be read as merely a switch being flipped on a track, an unintended deviation caused by, well, something. And these things will be well documented, as will the former. This is only and always a component of the archive. And this will only be another way of understanding the apocalypse.[73]

The story about rubber and oil companies buying up all the track in California, and subsequently ripping that track up so as to facilitate the rise and dominance of the automobile, is one that is familiar—we know it, it is old hat. It is a palpable mythology for anyone born east of the Mississippi. The entirety of "civilization" there has only been made possible with the increasing speed of transportation, whether rail, road, or air.[74] There is simply too much space, too much desert, too much wasteland to not see the train, and consequently its quite intentional replacement by the automobile, as an inevitability. Saying this isn't even interesting. Everyone knows this.

What makes this conspiracy so peculiarly interesting, however, is that this old story has an air of non-conspiracy around it, conspiracy as the type of foul air that pours out vulgar pastry shops and Stinkor's©[75] treated plastic, the type that emanates around such obvious blatant actions to pursue something like "progress" or the "march of history"—i.e., the conspiracy is so visible that it doesn't even seem worthwhile to comment upon, to descry, to condemn; there is something inevitable about these

---

[72] "Train Song I" lost, deleted, or misfiled.
[73] What I've also seen referred to as "Apocalypsapalooza."
[74] Tucson itself was originally (of course, after it was the home of the various residents displaced by the train and other horrors) merely a glorified railroad station. I used to live across the street from where the train men would shack up for a night. A couple of friends of mine used to live on the top floor of an old brothel (converted into apartments) that "serviced" those trainmen. The most popular nightspot is still Hotel/Club Congress, right across the street from the old/new railroad station, and on the other side was the Greyhound, now moved to a different, and potentially less convenient, location. Train-walking was one of our pastimes. I would hear it rumble through every night. The spot where we saw/played music had a backdoor that opened directly onto the tracks. Trains would rumble through in the middle of epic rock songs, only adding to the glorious din. Now the most important industries are Davis-Monthon Air Force Base and Raytheon (missile "systems"), the latter having employed a significant portion of my family and friends. Go figure. I suppose it doesn't need to be said that one could read here a certain "march of progress" ultimately ending in ever better ways of destroying things, in the ineluctable need to *move*.
[75] "The Evil Master of Odors." It is a little known fact that not only did He-Man suffer from bipolar disorder, but his nemesis Stinkor, once a boy named Odiphus, also had a severe case of "I-am-the-power"'s. It is terrible to yell at castles. They might move.

companies' actions that belies a kind of destiny. Furthermore, most of us like our conspiracies good and shrouded. The closed door, the Illuminati, the smoke-filled room, the Masons—these are "true" conspiracies because the means and aims surrounding them aren't clear; they attest to some veil of *māyā* pulled over the perception of the world's inhabitants, and if only it could be removed, things would be clear. The disappearance of the train lacks the sexiness, the swagger of this type of conspiracy, and yet the entire history of the locomotive is a romantic one. We owe much to this conspiracy and its palpable results.[76]

Maybe another way of approaching this is to recall the film *A Beautiful Mind* (2001), in which the brilliant mathematician played by Russell Crowe, though having conquered some esoteric mathematical problem, becomes completely embroiled in a schizophrenic world of conspiracy, of looking for *the answer* within every piece of text that comes along[77] and then stringing them together in a shack, pouring over each bit of the hyperarchive that he comes in contact with. Is it any wonder then that in *Children of Men* (2006) the protagonist is, at least to first impressions, locked up in such a room for questioning after being kidnapped? In this scene, we see Clive Owen being interrogated, but what really catches the eye[78] are the newspaper clippings on the wall: the tales of nuclear bombs, the decline of states, the acts of genocide. This is conspiracy in reverse. Something terrible has happened to the "human race" (they are unable to procreate), and the answer can only be found (for the viewer) in a shack much like Crowe's (notice the "sun" filtering in through the thin walls of the shack); and this shack now becomes the place of reverse-conspiracy and torture/interrogation. The subject upon whom a conspiracy is enacted (which is always "us," the preterite) now becomes the subject of interrogation, of the questioners'/conspirators' questioning, asking for answers from the very victim of their potential conspiracy. The fact that this façade is revealed to be false almost doesn't matter—i.e., it doesn't matter that this is merely a ploy by Julianne Moore's character to enlist Clive Owen in a cause (read: another conspiracy) and that simulating an interrogation room is the only way she could be sure she could "trust" him. This shack has been set up in what looks like an airplane hangar. False light is shone upon the walls of the shack to give the suggestion that it is outside. Why so much attention to detail beyond the obvious aesthetic advantages for the film in the form of textual proliferation? Why not simply a dark room with a lamp overhead? Why all this text?

---

[76] Though whether what we owe is worthwhile or not is in doubt.
[77] An action not so wholly different from what is(/has)/will occur(red) here.
[78] At least on the big screen.

There are other instances of rooms covered in text. One might think: of serial killer thrillers; or the James Joyce bar in Prague that has his writing exploding across the walls; of the stereotypical roadhouse/steakhouse with license plates covering everything[79]; of a teenager's room (mine) covered floor to ceiling with black-and-white copies of punk rock fliers, CD inserts, and adverts from *Maximum Rock-n-Roll*; of *23* (2007). These rooms always exist as sites of textual proliferation—unordered, semi-random, and mostly illegible to anything but the closest scrutiny. These rooms are overloaded with information to the point that, as in *Children of Men*, most of it remains inaccessible[80]—vision, reason, and the senses themselves cannot penetrate these archives. Pose this type of space against the gallery, the museum: our visual archives *par excellence*. What covers these walls exists in some, albeit arbitrary, order. The conspiracy of the gallery is of a different register. What Baudrillard calls "the conspiracy of art,"[81] might be said to be, in his terms, a conspiracy to simulate these other types of rooms, these other types of text that reveal a "real," though always uninterpretable, conspiracy.[82] (I hesitate to call what exists in galleries "texts" or other things that now go under that heading, but I think the analogy is clear.) These are formally sanctioned conspiracies, supported by the very nullity they themselves are simultaneously also trying to prop up,[83] as opposed to the textual space that is trying to *reveal* the conspiracy. The gallery space is of the same order as the conspiracy of the automobile. (It is apparent and need not be commented upon.[84]) Its visuality and the ability to stop anywhere and tarry awhile, mixed with incredible speed[85]—as opposed to being borne along, say, on a train whose stopping places are dictated, or the experience of a room whose

---

[79] The sheer randomness of all those numbers and codes suggests something very important about the archive of walls, about the automobile, about the disappearance of the train.

[80] The writers or set designers who manufactured all the newspaper articles should be commended. Their task was daunting. Nothing short of manufacturing a (textual) history that never occurred, an encyclopedia of apocalyptic destruction housed entirely in the imagination that no one would or could ever really read. Borges would be proud.

[81] See Jean Baudrillard, *The Conspiracy of Art*, ed. Sylvère Lotringer, trans. Ames Hodges (New York: Semiotext(e), 2005).

[82] Even if, say, the gallery space came first. They were always a response to rooms with text, even if these rooms hadn't appeared yet. See Thomas Hirschhorn's *Cavemanman* (2002).

[83] Much more work could be done around this issue, around the *space* in which text appears. (Still in the published city but not yet.) This, however, is slightly outside the purview of this appendix.

[84] It also doesn't really effect the enjoyment of those spaces (gallery, automobile). It even, one might hazard to say, heighten that enjoyment.

[85] Think of the National Gallery, where one can leap across a hall and go from the Medieval to the Dutch Renaissance.

stopping places are not apparent but give the illusion of a pattern, that they would be dictated if one could only read the schedule correctly—puts the subject/object of the conspiracy in a place where the conspiracy *ceases to be a visible conspiracy*, which is where the danger lies. If one can no longer even have the *illusion* that there are diabolical (or even deistic) Plans in place to control the world because these plans are so apparent—i.e., the stereotypical conspiracy-head investigating Marlon Brando's *Concord* can only be seen as "loony," "whacked," "not all there," because, well duh, all the conspiracies are right there in the open—then we are in a space/time where everything has already been revealed. The fact that the word "apocalypse" means revelation (in Greek: *apokalyptein*, to uncover, take the lid/veil off), a revealing of and a reveling in . . . (the end of time horrors), and that the *OED* stresses its second (and last) definition of the word, that apocalypse "is by extension: *any* revelation or disclosure," point toward a disturbing fact: that the apocalypse has already taken place. Yes, this is a difficult thesis to support, and *yes* there are still things that haven't been revealed, but the things that *humans* can hide and the *human* things that can be revealed are dwindling to the point where conspiracies as *simulacra* are now popping up, and on the opposite side, as in *A Beautiful Mind*, genius must absorb itself in *false* conspiracies because the real ones have no substance anymore—i.e., who really cares that the automobile companies ripped up all the railroad track?

This is also the genius of the ambiguity at the end of Umberto Eco's *Foucault's Pendulum* (1988): it is not, and cannot be made clear in the course of the narrative, whether the conspiracy the main character has stumbled upon is real or not. He has been implicit in its creation, and the ceremony he sees at the end is either "real" or merely its participants playing out the fantasy of conspiracy now that the "conspiracy" has no substance anymore. One might also think of Paul Auster's recent *Travels in the Scriptorium* (2007), in which the protagonist is literally imprisoned by the conspiracy text he himself has created, and because of lapses in his memory, cannot escape. The *illusion* of the conspiracy causes him to create it. The fact that it doesn't exist at all imprisons him.[86] One final, and most prescient example, might be read into the film *Memento* (2000). Because the character keeps forgetting everything every few minutes, he must literally transform his body into a text, signifying what he is supposed to "remember" so he can find the man who killed his wife. This *need* to remember, to *reveal*, enables less reputable characters to take advantage of him to do their dirty work, so that he ends up killing all sorts of people (implied). The key link in all of these examples is the role *text* plays in

---

[86] Though he does, strangely enough, get a hand-job out of the deal.

them—text inevitably creating conspiracies, real or imagined, that are *incredibly* more engaging than the conspiracies we already know about.

To posit an engaging and potentially productive thought experiment: the biblical, Revelations-type apocalypse has already occurred. And not only already occurred, but occurred a long time ago.[87] Yes, the 144,000, or whatever the relatively small number of those who were predestined for salvation, were Raptured. Think if this happened in like 500 CE or so. If this type of rapture occurred in the semi-ancient world, what would that look like? Maybe a villager or two would be missing. In the bigger cities, a few people. Humanity was relatively spread out, so even 144,000 departed souls might not even be *noticed* in the general scheme of things. It would be a small-scale, quiet apocalypse. Now the real seed of this thought experiment is: what happens if anyone notices? Who would notice? Who had the power to communicate with enough disparate groups of people to realize that all of the stories of people gone missing happened at the same time? Why, the Roman Catholic Church, of course! What would this do for their *power*? On the one hand, it could undermine every last bit of authority they would ever have. On the other, this would be the ultimate conspiracy: the Rapture occurred and has been hidden from *everyone*; potentially, even the documents revealing it would have been destroyed. Consequently, one could then read the entirety of Western Civilization as the attempt to hide and cover up this event, not simply because "we" couldn't handle it, that it would destroy the reason to "go on living," or whatever other commonplaces one might throw at it,[88] but because hiding this would guarantee, for eternity (or else a really long time), the primacy of the Judeo-Christian tradition, based, as it is, so heavily on salvation. The best part, the church would never actually have to worry about the Rapture occurring. They would have free reign to preach a salvation that would never come. Something similar actually happened. The predicted apocalypse, for millennia now, kept *not happening*, so the Church kept pushing back the date, until Bede realized that the only way to ensure the prediction was to take literally the "but not yet." Otherwise, the Church's authority would not be based on anything people actually wanted. The productive part of this thought experiment lies in actually *believing* that the apocalypse already occurred, that this completely fictional tale is somewhat closer to "the way things are" than the other

---

[87] As opposed to the laughably scripturally inaccurate *Left Behind* (1995-2007) series, in which all good Christians go to heaven in its opening scene.
[88] Again, see *Children of Men* for the effects of a future with no hope of salvation.

version of the coming "end of days." Everything is always post-apocalyptic.[89]

Now that I have meandered on various paths, posited various absurd theses and theories (the work of a good conspiracy theorist, I suppose), and come to this point—what is the "use" of talking about conspiracy? None whatsoever. I am interested, far more, in the things that have always been at the margin of this discussion, namely trains and words. The nature of conspiracy is that everything can get in. Once one starts looking for it, they find it. It just so happens that trains have a peculiar relationship with conspiracy, and by relation of examples, so do texts. As in: one might find themselves in front of a text that makes frequent reference to trains—what is one supposed to "look for"? Is there anything to "find"? Take care, dear co-conspirator, how you make use of your own archive. They may know how I've made use of mine, with care.
. . .

---

[89] Or, no apocalypse, not now—possibilities for non-eschatological/teleological "travel" "narrative" in the hyperarchive—nomadology as hypertopian anticipatory illumination, etc., etc.

Appendix II: Looking Like This, Tonight

Massive catalepsy!
I've got dressed up like this
to rock. Half the night we
were nigh in between these strictures
moaning delirious convalescence to those
half-between the "Why are You Here!?"[90];
and the: *I'm* under the smokestack (and I don't
really care where you are) sniffing the dandelion
sheep. There is no reason for sentence hoar-frostery.
There are ice cream trucks. And Sokal[91]
may be beneath one. Knowing that any information herein
is unnecessary. The prunes may be back, yet no one
can tell you otherwise. This ain't my first rodeo.

What here? You are as lost as a ferret. No joke.
There are "three" things to look for:

1) Robert Heinlein hiding in the bushes.

2) Two railroad tracks and their convergence (get it? baseball, etc.).

3) Kender in the Abyss.

4) Wagner.

5) Sylar.

6) "The Heart Skip-Beat Mambo!"

7) The Mantra.

8) The object.

9) . . . [Here. Where everyone gets lost.
Pioneers came this way, see? There
was water then. There were roots
that didn't *only* have to spread out over
thousands of feet, and go down. "Defenestrate

---

[90] Tacked on as if to indicate the revolutionary "random act of kindness."
[91] See the *Social Text* affair.

Psychoanalysts." Pale fires only glow for so long.] . . . Mormons.
Books are insulation. Dangerous to smoke too many
cigarettes around them. Do you think there is one
Prelude here? Can I tell you what I made?
"They made me this way." Whose right was that
to throw the book at your noggin like so?
I'm tired.

10) Mono. The North Rim. Paducah. The Last Chance Saloon. TSFHSB. That mailbox.[92] The meteorites we never watched. Be still and know. Adorno. The "we gotta leave the planet" conversation. Sleepers. A night where everyone screamed my name. When something ends? Typing. The new beat. The pit and the devil and the spot to wait it out. Staring into the abyss from Mars. Little Armenia. Rocking chairs. Fractured ke-winky-dinks. Convents. Writing this archive. My last name. The cello.

The blind leading the seeing down an alley.
With no question of death at the end.

[93]

Ø

---

[92] Wink.
[93] Is sadness permitted?

ENDNOTES

The epigraph is drawn from Friedrich Nietzsche, *Also sprach Zarathustra: Ein Buch für Alle und Keinen*, ed. Peter Pütz (1891; repr., Munich: Goldmann, 1999), 128. This has been translated as: "'Behold,' I continued, 'this moment! From this gateway, Moment, a long, eternal lane leads *backward:* behind us lies eternity. Must not whatever *can* walk have walked on this lane before? Must not whatever *can* happen have happened, have been done, have passed by before? And if everything has been there before—what do you think, dwarf, of this moment? Must not this gateway too have been there before? And are not all things knotted together so firmly that this moment draws after it *all* that is to come? Therefore—itself too? For whatever *can* walk—in this long lane out *there* too, it *must* walk once more'" (*Thus Spoke Zarathustra: A Book for All and None*, trans. Walter Kaufmann [1954; repr., New York: Modern Library, 1995], 158).

[a] Xavier right to become Onslaught, Žižek right to reference Heinlein: both Malevichian blots, both utopian dreams up against Sade, former and latter: singing, "Kafka on the Shore, Kafka on the Shore"; and those two chords ring sine-wave friendly over this easy hypotenuse.

[b] As was Kurtz (observed by one Marlow and another). Rather, pleonasty, prolixia, *rolling-up*: much like a recent Japanese videogame, *Katamari Damacy* (2004), whose basic premise is that you begin as an atom and proceed to "roll-up" and absorb the world until you and it cannot be distinguished. In the game you become not only the *objet petit a*: the stars have been destroyed and the only way to make the sky whole again, to cover up its lack, is to "roll-up" the things on Earth, but, strangely enough, the roll-up becomes, by extension of this object's absorbing principle, the whole, the Plotinian One: all else emanating from it, consequently creating an entire whole, a symbolic system that covers over the obscene fact that the roll-up is nothing more than the collected trash, symbols, and objects of the world through which the lack became apparent. To follow the title of a book by Theodor W. Adorno, *Stars Down to Earth* (trans. 1994), what has come down now must literally go back up, not as stars, but as accumulated cultural refuse (even people are rolled-up and sent into space, which seems the height of reification, not to mention the most terrible apocalyptic moment: the world, nay, the universe is destroyed by this action, but that destruction is a return to an original singularity, a One, the Real,* and nothing else [which could, in effect, reproduce the Big Bang (the pressure would be so great that it would have to explode/emanate), consequently being the para(/tanta)mount creative moment: destruction/creation, singularity/nothingness. . .]).*

> *One could here list a codex of terms that seem to share some basic kernel of the concept of the Real (or possibly the big Other), far before it was brought to its height in Lacanian terminology: Form and Idea in Plato, God, the Trinity in St. Paul, the sublime in Longinus, the One and the Intellectual-Principle in Plotinus, the Wheel of Fortune in Boethius, Satan trapped in ice in Dante, the Thing-Itself in Kant, the Nothing or Void in Nietzsche, transcendental *epochē* in the phenomenology of both Husserl and Heidegger, the Horror in Conrad, an Aesthetic Shudder in Adorno, the Aura in Benjamin, all the way down to Big Brother or a Terrorist, the hyperarchive, etc., etc. (not to mention the "footnote-itself," nor Truth). My point here is not so much to understand the Real (or any of these really) by the substitution of terms, but rather that the sheer inability of the term *the Real* (or any of these) to resist such substitutions becomes a methodology all its own. So I lied. There is some shred, some semblance of method for I (surely) am no Kurtz.

[c] "After nature had drawn just a few more breaths the planet froze and the clever animals had to die" (Friedrich Nietzsche, "On Truth and Lying in a Non-Moral Sense" [1873], in

The Birth of Tragedy and Other Writings, ed. Raymond Geuss, trans. and ed. Ronald Speirs [New York: Cambridge University Press, 1999], 141).

d "Coffee spreads darkness" (Friedrich Nietzsche, *Ecce Homo* [1908], in *Basic Writings of Nietzsche*, trans. and ed. Walter Kaufmann [New York: Modern Library, 1968], 695).

e And at this point a distinct chapter has ended: "I didn't have as much time as I thought to get to work, but Charlie will take you home. It was a pleasure, as always, to have you back, and for this week I felt a little more sane than I have been in a while. I am making plans to hit New England this summer, so we must stay in touch. Write me when you get back so that we can start our correspondence. I'll get to work on either something about Conrad or Saint Paul." —Sean Anderson, on a torn slip of yellow writing-pad paper, Sunday, 22 May 2005, after a quiet nite of [redacted].

f The answer to this question, sadly, lies not so deeply lodged on the first page of *The Golden Bough* (Frazer's 1922 abridgement): "In this sacred grove there grew a certain tree round which at any time of the day, and probably far into the night, a grim figure might be seen to prowl. In his hand he carried a drawn sword, and he kept peering warily about him as if at every instant he expected to be set upon by an enemy. He was a priest and a murderer; and the man for whom he looked was sooner or later to murder him and hold the priesthood in his stead. Such was the rule of the sanctuary. A candidate for the priesthood could only succeed to office by slaying the priest, and having slain him, he retained his office till he was himself slain by a stronger or craftier [. . .]. Within the sanctuary at Nemi grew a certain tree of which no branch might be broken. Only a runaway slave was allowed to break off, if he could, one of its boughs. Success in the attempt entitled him to fight the priest in single combat, and if he slew him he reigned in his stead with the title of King of the Wood" (James Frazer, *The Golden Bough: A Study in Magic and Religion*, abr. ed. [New York: Penguin, 1996], 1, 3).

g Michael Agnes, ed., *Webster's New World College Dictionary*, 4th ed. (Forest City, CA: IDG Books Worldwide, 2001), 265. On a "side" note: this is no substitute for the *Handy-Dandy Rand McNally*, in terms of reference books. On another side note, the aforementioned fourth was recommended to me by one "kind" of replacement, and that is why I have been so faithful to it. That is saying really nothing for the ninth, however.

h "Our citations, taken from more than twenty-five poets, from Spenser to Longfellow, will show how general has been the practice of borrowing illustrations from mythology" (Thomas Bullfinch, preface to *Bullfinch's Mythology* [New York: Gramercy, 2001], v). And we would here desire to say the same damn thing about rock music.

i Another note on methodology (warning: this does not assume that there is any such thing as a unitary subjectivity/authorship available or offered in this disclaimer, *nor* is this some kind of false pretense/play with which to criticize and/or complicate exactly what is going on [*a la* Vladimir Nabokov's *Pale Fire* (1962)]. No, this is something else): As en. b discusses (see page 109), there is a haziness, a finicky indeterminacy regarding the general question of methodology at work in the present moment. The infinite substitution, the *hermēneús* of naming, of objectifying what absolutely resists this type of work *is* a concern, *a* methodology here. But in introducing this type of "rolling-up," there exists a necessity, or at least an urge/drive/object-of-desire for dialectical play, but dialectical in the sense of locating the parallax gap (thus the title and placement of the above)—basically, to pose the opposite type of work/methodology against the *katamari* with the understanding that it is merely another way of looking at the same thing, the other side of the coin (but the same coin). What this opposite action is need not be stated in detail, since, if it is the same action only viewed through another lens, then it wouldn't make any sense to look at it as *opposite* at all. No, what is of interest here is what *resists* this methodology. And in danger of becoming a methodology in-itself, even the act of resisting must be resisted. So this need be stated with some amount of precision, clarity, or at least a level of self-awareness, and comes at a moment when this statement can now finally be made, since the gambit, the opening, the initial *essai* has occurred. Waffling no longer available, certain things now "written in stone" (as much as anything can be in this electronic medium . . .), the dice having been definitively rolled, *reason* (as in: "I" am not trying to give a "reason" for what is appearing) is exiting slowly but being retained, like the film left over on one's skin after a shower when the lather was not rinsed off (warning: beware the cleansing/redemptive aspect of this metaphor—danger lies ahead in doing so), and the proliferation of a different kind of "logic" now occurs.

To be clear. When She transcended/destroyed, what was enacted by the constellation that comes under the heading "Bardo Lièr Parté" was the fantasy-play of phantasmagoric imagination fulfilled, the object-cause of desire fully explicated, i.e., the *über*-"Grand Narrative"—the Angel of History taking stock, the messianic push redrawn in hyperarchivable, twenty-first-century-grammatological terms—enacted itself. This standard narrative had to occur so that it could be upset, and it had to occur as complete simulacra. It had to create itself, not having a common (or any) referent other than its own act of creation: parthenogenesis. "Had," however, is, of course, problematic. It assumes a ground, and more importantly, a ground of/by/for necessity that has no veracity—but there must be something at stake here (again, possibly only itself, which is merely the smuggling in of a desire for Ø to do mimetic work). This is all to say that the Event was a death, the death of the inhabitant of the Rocking Chair, but this event is two-fold. The second part of this initiatory Event (that is *not* an origin) is its own coming into veracity by the faithful act of telling a narrative so that it need not be told again. This narrative—which is always simultaneously its own dissipation, enacting its own nullity, happening only to not happen—"has to happen" because "The One" *must* be dealt with, on its own terms, in its own realm(s), so that the multiple can come into play, the multiple that this whole thing is, the poetic multiple: "the poem cleans[ing] language from within by slicing off the agency of loss and return. That is because we have lost nothing and nothing returns. . . . Committed to the triple destitution of the gods, we, inhabitants of the Earth's infinite sojourn, can assert that everything is here, always here, and that thought's reserve lies in the thoroughly informed and firmly declared egalitarian platitude of what befalls upon us here. Here is the place where truths come to be. Here we are infinite. Here nothing is promised to us, only to be faithful to what befalls upon us" (Alain Badiou, *Briefings on Existence: A Short Treatise on Transitory Ontology* [1998], trans. and ed. Norman Madarasz [Albany: SUNY Press, 2006], 31). To take a cue from the scrivener (who is "the distinctive living infinity arranged under the phrase ['Bartleby']" [25]), the narrative, even within its own coming into being, veracity, and faith, is ultimately a statement of "I'd prefer not to." "Freedom," or what falls under the infinite multiple the term designates, the ability to let the multiplicity of utterances become in-themselves outside the myth of originary unity, will(/choice/agency), and now something loosely assembled under the heading "creation"—these are the attentive, faithful results, and cause a loosing of the constraints of the dominating discourse of the One and the narrative it implies (thus an expunging and simultaneous embrace of the infinite substitution and/of naming)—this is the opening/closing of dealing with certain "philosophies of history." And having thus occurred, something like vision or proliferation happens/becomes available.

Lastly, it need be noted here precisely where "we" are. The vision offered is one in which the infinity of the void is the only vision. Or to be more precise, *apocalyptics be*. This is not metaphysical apocalypse. This is not religious apocalypse. This is not a "third way," "middle way," or synthesis. This is the gap: what does not come under the heading of apocalypse but is merely a manner of stepping outside itself. This is the vision that will now allow multiplicity, proliferation, rhizomatic effluvia, the "personal" or "individual"; this is what will allow the investigation of time under a distinctive heading to occur and go forth; this is the opening onto the play of the diabolic, the investigation of the index, the immersion in the ocean, the desert, and ultimately, the construction of railroad tracks to allow this journey to continue on whatever paths, linear or not, it wishes to—which is all that is available. The summer is waiting for our sinking and travel, our outpouring.

[i] **Oceanic II**

Your faith . . . is striated. Like porcelain wine.
When I'm counting amethysts, accidentally,
your faith becomes centripetal movement
betimes a lasting Colander Grill; in the night
your faith is becalmed upon a soft petaled requiem.
And I read between the misers. This fickle fidelity
tends toward the smashing and grabbing kind
of haunches we are enlimbered by. Perhaps a Notting
bug. Christine Christine. Your makeout parties
were quite short of pristine, Christine. We shot the animals
there with human tranquilizers, full of lead paint and diarrhetic.
My faith is "my dead grandmother clambering up a wall
with an [insert] in her mouth." This was merely the Fireman's
Ball pre-melee voluntarism taken to task. "Take out the pins,"
your book said to you, and we complied, miss sass, the—
dadgummit—motion crept along the sides of the sea.
Faith didn't drown but was washed along.
A catapult for tomorrow's orgies in the sea.

[k] St. Paul: . . . I don't think you understand. I am nothing more
than a coffin waiting patiently on a divan, for
the wisdom of the wise—

Oprah Winfrey: Is nothing more than the equation of this salon!
To host . . . the Hanford Village Annual BBQ . . .
what sublime treats must be waiting for me
in the quarantined afterlife to warrant such
opulent and radiant. . . .

Theodore Roosevelt, Jr.: The studs in my arms are gleaming shoehorns of change:
whittled and mottled dark angioplasty in the corpse-den of
    tomorrow.
Lament gross and incomparable (need, not heroics, but
    libertinage; nostrums passing by
the way to normalcy and revolution coming unhinged by
    this filial restoration—not
agitation but adjustment, surgery and serenity!—
    dispassionate experiments on equitable
mindscapes, but equipoise and submergence in
    internationality sustains a triumphant
nationality . . .).

St. John the Apostle: "Imagine! Two dozen sales clerks valiantly holding off the
    barbarian hordes! I hope
those poor children don't get hurt."

Emma Lazarus:	The picto-jumping box, I saw it all! The heads and horns, the cuneiform skywriting! My patronage has outgrown its own . . . auto-pontifications! From where? From what grand opera house does this ball-shriveling light come from?
Retarded Baby Jesus:	From my crown. From my future wounds. What of it, he for whom Marlow . . . ?
Marlon Brando:	No! Stop the cutting gibe of your own mistakes. Look into the sky. Look. Forever upward the light takes its falling inconsistencies—
Kurt Gödel:	Nigh incompleteness—
René Magritte:	No, an apple and a room—
Marlon Brando:	to the drifting house of mafia and sex . . . if you let the worms get inside you.

[1] *Chronicles of Riddick, A Canticle for Leibowitz, Organs of Megadeth, The Road, The Annotated Chronicles and Legends, Koyaanisqatsi, Infinite Jest, eXistenZ, The Matrix, Train Song I, The Broom of the System, The Terminator, Children of Men, Blindness* and *Seeing, Endgame,* CNN, *The Book of Dave, Just a Couple of Days, End Time, Accelerando, Dhalgren, Childhood's End, House of Leaves, Specimen Days, White Noise,* American Idol, *The Earth Abides, Alas, Babylon, Counter-Clock World, The Name of the Rose, Katamari Damacy, Lucifer's Hammer, The Stand, The Illusion of the End,* "Europe," *Calculating God, Most of the Time We Get Off the Planet Alive, Terra Nostra, Misappropriated Nukes,* ARGs, *Carpenter's Gothic, Left Behind, On the Beach, Armageddon, Deep Impact, Independence Day, The World Without Us, War of the Worlds, Last and First Men, The Last Man, Mars Attacks, Eschatology of the One and the Multiple, 28 Days Later, Fallout: New Vegas, I Am Alive, 28 Weeks Later, Resident Evil, Agent Zero, World War Z, Escape From New York, Pale Rider, High Plains Drifter, Dogville, Category 7, Reign of Fire, Mad Max, Jericho, Ruins: A Space Opera, Battlestar Galactica, The Age of Apocalypse, The Day After Tomorrow, God of War III, The World Doesn't End,* "The Waste Land," *the descent of ALEfTE, The New World, The Shadow Train, State of Decay, Angel Dust Apocalypse, Ridley Walker, The Wheel of Time, Nomads, Planet of the Apes, Star Road, The Lathe of Heaven, Final Fantasy VI, Southland Tales, The Age of Deterrence, Lost, Apocalypto, 2012,* Wikipedia, *Hard-Boiled Wonderland and the End of the World, Parable of the Sower, Oryx and Crake, The Hitchhiker's Guide to the Galaxy, Dr. Strangelove; or: How I Learned to Stop Worrying and Love the Bomb, Travels in the Scriptorium, The Wild Shore, LA's Destiny, Atlas Shrugged, The Beginning and the End, Red Dawn, Gravity's Rainbow,* "Last World," *The Last of Us, Dancing on the Ashes of Tomorrow, The FeMale mAN, We, Logan's Run, Möbius Visions, Hitler, ein Film aus Deutschland, Solaris, 2001: A Space Odyssey, The Wild Blue Yonder, La Jetée, 12 Monkeys, Mad Max: Beyond Thunderdome, Nuclear Attack! A Game of Strategy, Fun, and Survival, Dark City, Akira, News from Nowhere, Time's Railroad, The Inferno, On a Winter's Night a Traveler,* Amazon.com, *America, Thus Spoke Zarathustra, My Love Story in the Hyperarchive, The Moon is a Harsh Mistress, Le temps du loups, Wall-E, The Day the Earth Stood Still, The Happening, Doomsday, Until the End of the World, I Am Legend, Apocalypse Now, The Invasion of the Body Snatchers, Stalker, The Sacrifice, Idiocracy, Sunshine, Underworld, The Omen, The Falls, Anathem, Watchmen, Foundation, Spring and All, Blood Music, Farnham's Freehold, Drakengard, Fallout 3, The Dark Phoenix Saga, End Zone, Satanic Verses, Revelations, The (Dis)Union Pacific,* etc., etc.

[m] **Yet Another Destroyer and the Tale of that Destruction (In the First Person)**

Somewhere there may be a bit of commotion
flanked along its backside by a burning castration.
An expansive empire of strange galactic symmetry
mainlined into and feeding on angel blood—somewhere
there is not the slightest fiction of its demise but of its
coming to pass.

It has been far easier for me to divorce my own fraternity
so as to escape amongst the gaping cosmic infinities rather than
ease this body into citizenry. "Canada, oh Canada,
I've never been your son." I am a celestial, surfing
the regions inaccessible to my kind. I am no ambassador
or herald. Galactus holds no sway in this consciousness.

"I left on a stormy, balmy day in August from one of the many suburban regions in Western Pennsylvania. The day had started off like most others, but by the time I got to work, I was irradiated, glowing, and threatening to lay waste to the land from Chicago to the Eastern Seaboard. Turning off my car, I collected myself, hoping to end the hallucination that was allowing me to see my bones through my own skin, to simply make it into the mill to continue yet another punch-in/punch-out (rent was a month late). The next thing I knew, I was soaring past stars, navigating the universe as if it were memory, consuming suns and worlds with less compunction than ease."

From whence did I rise? And was it foretold in any
of the many annals and archives dotting the known
and unknown universe?

There is no need to tell my tale. There
are none to hear who would believe, at least among
the living, so I can go very quickly
with no need to pause upon any significant detail,
and yet . . . here I am, still no end in sight, though
sprung from one of the few races
who will probably destroy themselves before leaving.

No, yet another cosmic accident, another purposeless sublimity
and transcendence. And in the blink of an eye, Terra is gone.
Someone called "I" continues.

[n] Excerpt beginning at *of course* from Richard Cole, *Stairway to Heaven: Led Zeppelin Uncensored* (New York: Harper, 1992), 288.

[o] The only lyrics to "IRC to the CIA" by Milemarker on their album *Changing Caring Humans: A Collection of Compilation Songs and Singles* (Atlanta, GA: Stickfigure Records, 1999). Written in the liner notes of the collection is an account of their activity: "As word spread, and (as is the nature of words) solidified into the formal language of labels and clichés, the collective only veered more wildly, confounding audiences searching for rote and predictability with performances conducted behind blank screens, video projections of simultaneously teleconferencing band members, and concerts carried out entirely by automated robots of the group's devising. . . . Manifestos and footnoted reference guides to the philosophical and political undercurrents of these shows were distributed in such

volume that truly diligent followers of the group soon found themselves too busy underlining important passages to attend the performances themselves."

p Martin Heidegger, *Being and Time: A Translation of "Sein und Zeit"* (1927), trans. Joan Stambaugh (Albany: SUNY Press, 1996), 35. "Led Zeppelin" inserted for Heidegger's term for the being of beings: *Dasein*, not to be confused with Being or existence. Certain parts omitted.

q Bury [my heart at wounded knee (. . . and)] Me Standing, "Hope as a Cure for Suffocation," *Empires Today, Ashes Tomorrow* (Tucson, AZ: Code of Ethics Records, 1999).

r "Blippity bop. Blippity bop. This is why I walk and talk this way" (DJ Shadow, "Fixed Income," *Private Press* [New York: Universal/MCA Records, 2002]). P.s. ("Those needles start to drop. Tomorrow never comes until it's too late. . . . It's April Fool's Day"), quietude!

s How much will be written about Phillip Glass in the twenty-third century? (Singing, "Einstein on the beach. Einstein on the beach.")

t Or maybe more appropriately, to paraphrase Neil Young, digitized music sounds like ice-cubes falling in a glass rather than the pure analog flow of water, which contains no breaks other than sloshing, and because of that, more gently resembles the reality (if one can hopefully call it that) of what we are experiencing.

u Walter Benjamin, "Paris, the Capital of the Nineteenth Century" (1935), in *The Arcades Project*, trans Howard Eiland and Kevin McLaughlin, ed. Rolf Tiedemann (Cambridge, MA: Belknap Press of Harvard University Press 1999), 3. This is not to de-calculate the messianic nature of miscalculation.

v J. R. Ewing. Also see "Laughing with Daggers." So loud and no distortion. So many amps. Enjoying being full-time assholes. *Calling in Dead.*

w "If you fake the funk, your nose will grow" (Bootsy Collins).

x Interstellar Sirius Radiatio.

y A star system. Coordinates unknown. Believed to be using some hyper-bandwidth cloaking device. Huge coup upon treaty 0.8473.9583729.bh85.astro.beelzebub.con.

z Galactic Intellect Quotient.

aa Aura-Filled Moments of Clarity Dominating the Association Processor [AFMCDAP (what might be called memory, but with quotations)].

bb Please file under: C:\Documents and Settings\Owner\My Documents\The Hyper-archive\multi-media\ALL WRITING DOCS\poetry\poetry 4 fall 06\12 5 Synchronic Record Review. Password: promontorygoldenspike.

cc I despise putting this code (Were/Was Especially Interesting): my subject was given to me by the conglomerate.

dd This matter under consideration is currently available at the above location, with added post-script: Incidental/Audio/tunes.

ee When the *Pequod* becomes a starship and the Pacific becomes a slightly altered, slightly smarter, Crab Nebula.

ff Evident in *Wicker Man* (1973), but (surely) other places as well: "With *carnivalistic folklore* [. . .]—saturated with a specific [oral] *carnival sense of the world* [. . .] permeating [. . .] genres from top to bottom, [this] determines their basic features and places image and word in them in a special relationship to reality. [. . .] This carnival sense of the world possesses a mighty life-creating and transforming power, an indestructible vitality. [. . .] The sensitive ear will always catch even the most distant echoes of a carnival sense of the world" (Mikhail Bakhtin, *Problems of Dostoevsky's Poetics*, ed. and trans. Caryl Emerson [Minneapolis: University of Minnesota Press, 1984], 107). It would not be a stretch, surely not an elasticity[!], to condemn, approach, commend this here trite and humble author to the [obvious] affinities and ease in which M[etal]. B[lade]. [records] could here support/ befuckingastoundedby: polyphonics is for *narrative*. But then, I suppose the circling would get very tiresome. (Imagine running a marathon on a quarter-mile track. Yeesh.) *Nevermind* (an entertainer).

gg I am coming unraveled and finding little solace in the wisdom: beat your megaphones into ear-trumpets. What medium, what possible instrument, machine, lexical-device could bridge the gap (not talking theologically) between my (or anyone else's for that matter) "voice" and what I hear on the tape? So many directions, handbooks, guides. . . . To write, to instruct, to explore . . . *was*? The most valid workings of (in)action are the seepings away, the gradual destructions of whatever passed for confidence. Arrogance, not its own destructor, but the attempt to curb, is.

hh I, for one, have always been (up until the present moment) more "affected" by the droning vibrations that come under the heading of "music" (nowadays), than anything else. Did Mono and Black Dice, seeing them, weeping in their temporality and complete ignorance of beauty, their destruction, their "will to nothing" . . . did these things ruin the very fabric of ear-space that I, for so long, had valued above all? What in its stead has been inserted? *A Broken Ear Record* indeed. . . .

ii And no not "NAVY SEALS." The videogame/propaganda/culture-of-violence/mistaken identity/sim-u-la-tio*n* that is, in effect, nothing more than Training for Utopia—this *is* the training we need, but (surely) not in this form. . . .

jj I had mislaid my watch. Finding it, holding it close to my ear, I realize it is not in step. One gear has lost one atom, one neutrino, and measurement must be recalibrated, turned ahead a few minutes, back, forth, wait for the second-hand . . . but the sun is always moving, but the years are not divided well, but the leap. . . . It is   now   always a bit fast.

kk No negative force either. Losing the proverbial 22 does not constitute incontestable materiality (though good luck looking anywhere else for this). The relationship between Armageddon and death is flimsy. There, but flimsy. The problem: there is always a post-apocalyptic moment, even if a glimmering (until the Big Crunch, I suppose. But all that smashing, it'd be like a super-bouncy-ball, would just spring back, beginning anew), there is not, however, a conceivable afterlife (not requiring faith) except in memory, which is as fallible as someone raging against anything, let alone the dying . . . of mi(dni)ght. (I do not require you to agree with me on this one.)

ll The beauty of consumption is that it inevitably turns into waste. Eating *is* a creating, both shit and fuel. At the heart of "modern" consumption lies some fuel, but it is like calling opium fuel. This does not mean opiates are unnecessary. Too quickly we see the derogative nature of escaping. No one has ever "judged" dreams. We have only attempted to interpret them. A bad dream is nothing more than one that leaves us with a disagreeable interpretation.

ACKNOWLEDGMENTS

Portions of this book have been previously published in slightly different forms:

"Oceanic," in "Sci-Pulp Poetics," special issue, *PELT*, no. 3 (September 2014), 52-53, http://organismforpoeticresearch.org/two-poems-bradley-fest/.

"If the Marianas Trench Were a Gathering of Sound," *After Happy Hour Review*, no. 1 (March 2014): 22, http://afterhappyhourreview.com/.

"Two Parts of a Parallax Gap[1]," *Flywheel Magazine*, no. 2 (January 2012), http://www.flywheelmag.com/962/two-parts-of-a-parallax-gap%C2%B9/.

"A Second E(ff)luvium," *BathHouse* 8, no. 1 (February 2011), http://www.bhjournal.net/.

"Nothingness Introduced into the Heart of the Image," in *Open Thread Regional Review*, vol. 2, ed. Cecilia Westbrook (Pittsburgh, PA: Open Thread, 2010), 53.

"The One/Symphony of the Great Transnational," *Spork* 6, no. 1 (Summer 2007), http//www.sporkpress.com/6_1/pieces/Fest.html.

Thanks to the many friends, interlocutors, readers, teachers, students, bandmates, and publishers who have helped me shape this book over many years and who are too numerous to name individually. Specific thanks must go to Sean Anderson, Taylor Baldwin, Ryan Bell, Don Bialostosky, C. M. Burroughs, Sten Carlson, Adam Chiles, Robin Clarke, Toi Derricotte, Jaxun Doten, Charles Engebretson, Lynn Emanuel, Eric Fest, Ian Finch, Mike Good, Paul Kameen, David James Keaton, Brendan Kerr, Valerie Krips, Stephen M. Llano, Jake Levine, Tiffany Marriman-Preston, Sara Marsh, Dean Matthews, Jonathan Moody, Haley Myers, Rachel Nagelberg, Tenney Nathanson, Shelagh Patterson, Alexander Provan, Daniel C. Remein, Gustavo Romero, Charles Sherry, Richard Siken, Philip E. Smith II, Tracy K. Smith, Kurt Sommer, Mark Sussman, Michael Thomas Taren, Bill Tsitsos, Michael Upton, and Joshua Zelesnick. This book would not have been possible without the generosity, enthusiasm, and encouragement of Tomaž Šalamun; he will be missed. Thanks also to the editors of the journals in which some of these poems first appeared. I would like to express my sincerest gratitude to Adriana E. Ramirez, Jesse Welch, and Blue Sketch Press for finally bringing this book into the light of day. The warmest thanks to my family, and particularly my mother for giving me the support to realize this project. And always, to Racheal, my dynamo.

ABOUT THE AUTHOR

Bradley J. Fest teaches literature as a Visiting Lecturer at the University of Pittsburgh. At present he is working on *The Nuclear Archive: American Literature Before and After the Bomb*, a book investigating the relationship between nuclear and information technology in twentieth and twenty-first century American literature. His poems have appeared in *After Happy Hour Review*, *BathHouse*, *Flywheel*, *PELT*, *PLINTH*, *Open Thread*, *Spork*, *2River View*, and elsewhere. He has published articles in *boundary 2*, *Critical Quarterly*, and *Studies in the Novel*; and his essays have appeared in *David Foster Wallace and "The Long Thing"* (2014) and *The Silence of Fallout* (2013). He blogs at *The Hyperarchival Parallax*.

www.ingramcontent.com/pod-product-compliance
Lightning Source LLC
Chambersburg PA
CBHW021442080526
44588CB00009B/642